inside

The 10 communication secrets that will transform your business

Inside: the 10 communication secrets that will transform your business
Third edition: December 2017

© Matt Hampshire

Matt Hampshire has asserted his right under the Copyright, Designs
and Patents Act 1988 to be identified as the author of this work.
All rights reserved. No part of this book may be copied, stored,
transmitted or reproduced in any format or medium without specific
prior permission from the author or publisher.

Published by:
66 publications, The Forge, East Meon, GU32 1QD, United Kingdom

inside

Why you need to read this book	5
#1 What you do is more important than what you say	10
#2 It's not about you. It's about them	24
#3 Know yourself	37
#4 Start with the right people	55
#5 Have a good story (and stick to it)	67
#6 Turn down the background noise	83
#7 Make it simple	96
#8 Be interesting	113
#9 Be real	124
#10 Learn to let go	140
Making it happen	159

'If you want to build a ship, don't start by dividing up the work, collecting wood, cutting planks. Start by making your men yearn for the vast and endless sea'

Antoine de Saint Exupéry

'I still believe a car with the gas needle on empty can run about 50 more miles if you have the right music very loud on the stereo'

Hunter S Thompson

Why you need to read this book...

A long time ago, when I was younger and didn't know better, I used to work in advertising.

I worked with a lot of smart, funny people, I lived in some cool cities and I got to drink beer in the office. It felt like a pretty good way to earn a living.

There was just one thing about it that bothered me: the gap between what we promised in our ads and the actual experience people had when they bought some of our clients' products or shopped in some of their stores or stayed in some of their hotels.

When we'd talk about this with our clients, I was always surprised that they weren't more bothered. They'd shrug their shoulders and say something like 'Yeah – the Ops guys haven't really got behind this campaign.' As long as they were gaining more customers than they were losing, they didn't seem to mind.

But I did mind, because the ad I'd written had made somebody spend their money on something that hadn't lived up to the promise we'd made. I felt like a liar.

I was talking about this with some friends one day and we thought: why not set up an agency that would bridge this gap?

Our job would be to make sure the things our clients said and did on the inside of their business would match up with the promises they made to their customers on the outside. An agency focused on the experience of the brand, rather than the promise.

Technically, this made us an internal communication agency. When I told my friends in advertising what I was doing, they all thought I was crazy. They said: 'Really? Internal comms? But that's just so dull!'

Wow, I thought. These are very smart, switched-on people, who know all about persuasion, and they don't get it. They don't understand that even the most brilliant ad can't make up for a rubbish customer experience or a one-star online review.

Then I paused and thought: they're right, though. Internal communication is a bit dull. As soon as you start talking about it, peoples' eyes glaze over. They think of A4 newsletters, bullet points, intranets and pompous mission statements.

In fact, internal communication is so unsexy that a lot of companies don't even admit to doing it any more. They call it 'engagement' or 'connection' or 'employer brand'.

Yet the truth is that internal communication is one of the most important things your business does. It's the thing that allows you to deliver the promises you make in your advertising.

It doesn't matter what you call it. What matters is that, if you do it badly, your customers will probably have a bad experience. If you do it badly enough times, your business will fail.

Most businesses do it badly.

In the last ten years, customer experience has become the defining measure of a company's success. We live in a much more transparent world now: a world of peer opinions and online reviews, where your brand promises are only worth something if you keep them – and any failure to keep them becomes very visible, very quickly.

This is a world where you need to be able to rely on your people to make good decisions and yet they quite often don't. A world where technicians cheat emission tests to make car manufacturers' new models look better than they are. Where supermarket buyers squeeze suppliers into bankruptcy. Where utility company accountants send threatening demands to customers who died three months earlier. Where bank employees set up bogus accounts to help their customers dodge tax.

20 years ago, this kind of brand 'own goal' was all but invisible: a PR issue that could be managed and contained on the rare occasions when the noise grew loud enough. Now, it can be all over the internet by lunchtime – and, by the close of trading, your reputation (and share price) could have fallen off a cliff.

The only way to safeguard against it is to help your employees make better decisions. And the only way to do that is by being better at internal communication.

Sir Martin Sorrell (chief executive of advertising group WPP and arguably the world's foremost authority on business communication) recently described internal communication as 'the biggest challenge facing CEOs today.'

If you talk to most CEOs, there's a good chance they'll agree. There's an equally good chance they'll be frustrated by the way internal communication works in their own business.

In a recent survey by Deloitte, 92% of Chief Executives said they thought internal communication was critical to the success of their business. Only 28% thought their business was good enough at it.

In other words, 64% of Chief Executives are worried that their current internal communication is a business risk. They just don't know how to fix it.

That's what this book is about.

Over the last fifteen years, I've worked with a lot of different organisations and talked to a lot of CEOs. I've also talked to a lot of employees, communication specialists, advertising people, cognitive neuroscientists, teachers, comedians, sports coaches and military historians.

This book is a summary of what I've learned from all of them: the ten big things that will make your internal communication more effective and help your business succeed.

You'll recognise many of the same frustrations, the same symptoms and the same opportunities that you find in your own business. And you'll have a chance to learn from the brands and organisations that are getting it right.

I can't promise that you'll find the answers to all your problems in here.

But I can promise that you'll find the right questions.

Secret #1
What you do is more important than what you say

Twenty years ago, if we had a bad customer experience, we might have told our family and friends about it (an average of nine people, I remember some clever analyst had worked out).

If we have a bad customer experience today, half the planet can hear about it by lunchtime.

We're all publishers: we all have a voice and we no longer need to know someone who owns a newspaper to get that voice heard.

If you're a CEO, that thought is both terrifying and exhilarating. Terrifying, because one small mistake or misjudgement by one individual can have profoundly damaging consequences for your whole business. And exhilarating because it means that, if you do get something genuinely and distinctively right, the world really will beat a path to your door.

In other words, the rules have changed.

Brand success used to be mostly about what you said: the carefully-positioned image that you put across in your advertising and presentation.

Today, it's much more about what you do. Customers have access to a lot more information than they used to. And they're more likely to judge you by what other people say about you than by what you say about yourself.

In a recent survey, 90% of people said they would trust an online review from another customer, while only 14% said they would trust an advertising claim.

That's your problem.

The promise you make to customers – in your advertising, direct marketing, website, PR – all goes through a single filter (usually the Marketing Director, supported by a handful of carefully-selected agencies). So it usually feels quite joined-up. A clear message in a consistent voice.

But only 14% of your customers and potential customers are listening to that voice.

Whereas 90% of them are listening to the people who've already experienced your product or service. And the people who deliver that experience – your employees or agents – aren't as joined up as your marketing promise. They work in different departments, with different managers, often with different agendas and priorities and often at a significant geographical distance.

Some of them know what the right thing is to do for your

customers; some of them don't. Some of them care what your customers think; some of them don't. And your brand is only as good as the worst decision that any one of them makes.

So, what can you do to help make those decisions better?

People are your biggest asset. (No, really).

Imagine you've got a business that's full of people with a genuine shared purpose. People who all instinctively know how to put a smile on your customers' faces and more money on your bottom line – and who are enthusiastic about doing it.

Sounds good, doesn't it?

That's because you know the success of your brand or business depends on what customers think. And you also know that what customers think depends on your employees: what they do, what they say, how they behave.

Yet, if you were to map the engagement level of a typical employee in a FTSE100 company, it would look something like this:-

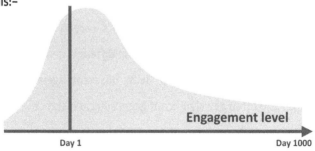

Not surprisingly, the high point of engagement is around the time an employee starts, or shortly afterwards. What you might call the honeymoon period. They're optimistic, excited: positive about the brand they're working for and full of the possibilities of what their new job will allow them to achieve. They're emotionally connected.

The problem is that most businesses are not very comfortable with emotion, because most businesses set out to work like machines.

Next time you're in an office, just pause for a moment and look at (or listen to) the way the business communicates: not just the channels – email, intranet, notice-boards – but management conversations, one-to-ones, performance reviews.

I'm willing to bet that what you see and hear will be very transactional. Lots of numbers, lots of facts, lots of 'hard measures', lots of process, lots of mechanistic language ('shifting gear', 'ironing out the kinks', 'the engine that drives growth').

I'm also willing to bet that you'll find plenty of confusion and inconsistency in the way those messages are expressed. Multiple priorities, with no clear hierarchy. Jargon and buzzwords. Variations in look and feel. And way, way too many words.

Over time, these things will take their toll on your new

employee's enthusiasm.

They remember that the business they joined *said* it prized simplicity – but they have to fill in three forms for every expenses claim.

They hear their Chief Executive *say* 'nothing is more important than our customers' – but all the measures in their performance review are about money.

When they turn on their computer every morning, there's a message on the company intranet *saying* 'your opinion matters' – but nobody's bothered to reply to the three ideas they submitted a month ago.

They hear the HR Director *say* 'we want to empower you' – but then they hear about a colleague who got fired for using their initiative, rather than following a process.

Before too long, the starry-eyed enthusiasm has vanished and your employee has learned to think in transactional terms, as well. They follow the process, they focus on the numbers. they become a compliant cog in the corporate machine.

But they don't feel particularly attached to the business any more – which means that, if someone makes them a better offer, you'll lose them.

And they don't really care about the experience your customers are having, unless it specifically affects their performance measures.

In other words, what most businesses are doing is taking motivated people and finding ways to de-motivate them.

The future belongs to companies that behave like humans

In the 1980s, when my Dad was working as a management consultant, he met a man called Jan Carlzon.

Carlzon was the CEO of SAS, the Scandinavian airline group, and is widely credited with turning around the group's fortunes through his policy of empowering front-line employees to take better decisions for customers.

The catalyst for this policy came shortly after Carlzon had taken over running the airline. The business had just reported a loss of $17m (quite a lot of money in those days). Carlzon was standing in line to get on one of his own flights, mentally wrestling with the problem of how to get SAS back into profitability.

The passenger in front of him had a problem of her own: she had to get to Stockholm in a hurry, but her ticket was for a later flight – could she change it? The clerk studied the ticket and politely explained to the passenger that the ticket wasn't just for a different flight – it was for a different airline. The passenger slumped in despair.

This was the point at which the clerk, having highlighted the error, should have politely directed the passenger over to the other airline's desk, where she would have waited in line and eventually found out that there were no earlier flights. That was the correct thing to do: it wasn't SAS's problem.

Instead, the clerk said: 'Don't worry. We've got space on this flight, so I'll just book you on it. I know the guys on the other airline desk: I'll sort it out with them.' He picked up the phone and did just that.

Carlzon thought: 'Hang on a minute: you've got no authority to do this – and no budget. What if the other airline won't compensate us?' But he didn't say anything. Instead, he allowed himself to keep looking at the situation through the eyes of a passenger, rather than the person ultimately responsible for the group's profitability.

He watched with interest as the passenger's mood changed from desperation to relief to gushing thanks. And he listened with even more interest as the passenger hugged the clerk and said words to the effect of: 'This is the best service I've ever had from any airline. I'm not even one of your customers – but I will be from now on.'

Carlzon described that as his 'Eureka' moment. He thought about it all the way home and realised that, if he could make all his staff more like that one clerk, he would have the happiest customers in the airline industry. And, if he had happy customers, he'd probably have a pretty successful airline. The next day, he called in his senior managers and started working out how they could encourage all their employees to make decisions that would make customers happy.

The following year, SAS went from a $17m loss to a $54M profit. They were named Airline of the Year – and they set up a training programme to teach other organisations (including competitors like British Airways) how to be better at Customer Service.

What I find really interesting about this story is how much of it is down to pure chance. What if Carlzon hadn't been in the queue that day and hadn't overheard the conversation? Would SAS have persisted with its centralised decision-making (and loss-making)? Would the check-in clerk have been disciplined for exceeding his authority – for not following the process? And, intriguingly, would British Airways ever have learned how to become the 'world's favourite airline'?

Perhaps not.

How can we help people make better decisions?

Shaun McIlrath is Creative Director at Iris, the UK's largest independent advertising agency. In a career spanning 30 years, he has advised many of the world's biggest brands. He says:

'The brands that are successful in the long term are the ones that behave like people. The ones that fail are the ones that show no people skills: they don't listen, they don't admit fault. It's all about them – and extracting money from you. You can only pull that off for so long before people lose interest in you.'

If you want your business to succeed, you have to make it really easy for people to know what the right thing is to do.

As an example of how to do it right, McIlrath cites Ocado, the online grocery retailer. When Ocado first launched in the UK, employees weren't given a long list of 'brand values'. They were given a picture of Father Christmas and told 'This is how we want customers to think of us.' A sweet and very clear statement of intent: crucially, on the inside rather than the outside.

'Lip service is the biggest problem,' says McIlrath. 'Companies want people to think that they're warm and helpful. But they don't always want to go to the trouble of actually *being* warm and helpful.'

Even when they do want to go the trouble, it doesn't always work out right.

Every day, in organisations all over the world, good people do bad things because they're distracted by financial incentives, because they're unthinkingly following a process or because they're influenced by what the people around them are doing.

Call centre operatives tell lies to people at the end of the phone.

Bank executives sell insurance to customers, even though they know they don't need it and won't benefit from it.

Shop assistants refuse to refund a broken product because the customer can't produce a receipt, even though they both know it came from their store.

Teachers exclude underperforming pupils, because they're being incentivised to hit challenging targets and don't want their averages reduced.

Airline check-in staff leave customers stranded miles away from their families, because they think they'll get in trouble if they help them get home.

The people who work in our organisations will keep making decisions like machines until we make it easier for them to behave like humans.

What's getting in the way?

As part of my job, I spend a lot of time talking to different people inside organisations, trying to work out why some of them are engaged with their jobs and most of them aren't.

What I've learned is that, in almost every organisation, there are three big things that get in the way: bad communication, bad processes and a lack of trust.

These are the things that stop people making good decisions – the things that result in a bad customer experience or a disappointing perception of your brand.

The following comments all genuinely come from conversations I've had with employees in client companies. Have a look and see if any of them sound familiar:

'There's too much noise in this business'

'It's hard to understand what the real priorities are'

'The values don't really mean anything'

'To be honest, I can't be bothered to read it'

'It's just corporate nonsense'

'What's it got to do with me?'

'I'm just here for the money'

'It'll all change again in six months'

'They say it's about customers – but it's really about money'

'There's no point using your initiative: just do what you're told and keep your head down'

'Boring!'

How many people in your own organisation do you think might be saying or feeling things like this? And, more importantly, what can you do about it?

Communication is the key to performance

Whenever you talk to HR people in any organisation, there's a good chance you'll hear them use the words 'high performance'.

They're describing what every organisation would like to achieve, but regrettably few do: the elusive combination of motivated people and consistent success.

You find examples of high-performing teams in almost any field: sport (Real Madrid, the All Blacks); the military (the SAS, US Navy Seals); cooking (Noma, el Bulli); retail (Nordstrom, Zappos, John Lewis).

They're all very different kinds of team, but they all share a number of the same characteristics:

The people in the team are highly engaged: they're proud of their history and proud to have earned their place in it.

They have a strong sense of identity and shared values.

They have clear goals – and they're very focused on achieving them.

They set high standards for themselves and their colleagues.

There's a high degree of trust: they know they can rely on the people around them.

Nothing especially insightful in any of that, you might think. They're the same characteristics any sensible and ambitious organisation would want to nurture.

And yet, when you sit and talk to the people in most organisations, you're less likely to recognise these characteristics – and far more likely to hear comments like the ones we identified on the previous page. Why?

Because those people don't have a clear sense of what the organisation stands for – which means they find it hard to know what the right thing is to do.

Because they feel restricted by process: they're so caught up in ticking boxes that they can't express their natural talent.

Because they don't work in an environment of trust, so they tend to focus their energy on looking after themselves, rather than working as a team.

In other words, the three key elements that differentiate high-performing teams from other teams are clarity, confidence and trust.

In all three cases, what makes the difference is how you communicate – which explains why 64% of CEOs don't think their internal communication is good enough.

Let's look at how we can make it better.

In a nutshell...

#1 What you do is more important than what you say

Only 14% of people would trust what you say about yourself as an organisation, whereas 90% would trust what others say about you. If you want your people to deliver a great customer experience, you need to make your organisation a place where people feel able to behave like humans, not like machines.

DO...

...make it easy for your people to make good decisions. This is about clarity (knowing the right thing to do), confidence (in their own ability) and trust (that you'll support them).

DON'T...

...confuse them with mixed messages, too much detail or conflicting priorities.

Secret #2:
It's not about you. It's about them

Dave Trott is one of the world's most respected advertising creatives.

He says 4% of all advertising in the UK is remembered positively, 7% is remembered negatively, and the other 89% isn't remembered at all.

That's pretty scary. The people who work in advertising are some of the smartest people you'll ever meet. If they can't make people interested in what they've got to say, what chance have the rest of us got?

The answer, of course, is that it's not about chance and it's not about how smart you are. The most important thing to remember about communication is that you can't talk to people who aren't listening.

If you look back at the memorable speeches in history – Kennedy's 'Man on the moon', Churchill's 'Fight them on the beaches' – it's striking how many people afterwards say 'it felt like he/she was talking just to me.'

Great orators have a gift for making their audience feel like they're speaking to them one on one. Even when they're in a stadium full of other people. Even when they're listening through a radio. Even if they're reading it on a page.

That's because all good communication feels like a conversation.

So, imagine that you're having a conversation with someone in a pub. What would you think if they only talked about themselves? Or if they seemed to be addressing the room in general? Or if they kept using long, made-up words that didn't make any sense? Or if they seemed to take themselves too seriously? Or if they just kept banging on and on and didn't let anyone else get a word in?

You probably wouldn't want to listen to them for very long.

Now, just pause for a moment and think about the communication inside your business. How much of it feels like a conversation – and how much of it feels like an impersonal information dump? How much of it is about the individual – and how much of it is about the business? Do the words sound natural and conversational – or do they sound stilted and formal? Is there any warmth, or humour? Is there actually any reason why someone would pay attention to it if they weren't being paid to?

Communicating inside a business is exactly the same as communicating anywhere else.

If you want people to listen to you, you've got to make it worth their while.

'What's in it for me?'

Most organisations approach internal communication in terms of what they want people to know. Here's our new strategy. How the new barcode system works. What are our priorities for the next three months?

There's nothing wrong with that, as long as you understand that your audience is not necessarily going to be interested in knowing it. And as long as you remember that you can't communicate with people who aren't listening.

If you *do* want your audience to listen, it might make more sense to start by thinking about them. Who are they? What are they interested in? Where do they usually like to get their information from? What do they chat about with their friends?

That doesn't mean you need to stop talking about your business priorities and start talking about Reality TV. It just means you need to look for ways to make your business priorities feel more relevant to your audience and their lives.

The more you can make the thing you want people to know feel like a thing they'd be interested in knowing, the better the chance your communication will work.

That's how successful advertising works. It draws people in. It charms them. It creates a sense of relationship. It paints a picture of how their life could be better if they were to buy whatever it is you're selling.

What it doesn't do (except in the worst kinds of infomercial) is hector them with clumsy propaganda. Or batter them repeatedly over the head with a wet sock full of facts that have no obvious connection to their lives.

If you want your workforce to listen to what you've got to say, you need to start by thinking about why they would want to listen.

As Walt Disney put it: 'We entertain people in the hope that we can educate them, because the other way round doesn't work.'

Your audience is changing

Workforces are increasingly made up of people born after 1982: the so-called 'Millennials'.

Experts are divided about the characteristics that define this generation. Descriptors vary from 'civic-minded', 'can-do' and 'social conscience' on the one hand, to 'narcissistic', 'entitled' and 'generation me' on the other.

What's certain is that Millennials are much more comfortable with the idea of change than previous generations. They grew up with digital technology and the internet – they've been involved in shaping it and expect to have a voice.

They're also a lot more confident: better informed, wider travelled, more willing to challenge authority and the status quo.

If you look at the senior management positions of the world's leading businesses, they're mostly made up of Baby Boomers (born before 1964) or Generation X (born mid-60s to early-80s). You won't yet find many Millennials among them (the glaring exception being Silicon Valley – which, not coincidentally, seems to be the source of most of the interesting cultural ideas shaping the way organisations work).

This generation gap creates a potential communication problem at two different levels.

Logistically, because the ways that Baby Boomers and Generation Xers like to communicate are not necessarily the same ways that Millennials like to receive information.

And culturally, because there is often a significant difference in world view between the generations. Generation Xers tend to be more transactional in their outlook ('I'll do it as long as you pay me enough'), while Millennials are more likely to be swayed by factors such as social purpose, community and responsibility.

When the people setting the business agenda are Generation Xers and many of their employees are Millennials, it's easy to see how this might lead to a breakdown in communication. So, how do you bridge the gap?

King Adz is one of the world's leading experts on youth communication and culture. An advertising creative by training, he has spent the last 15 years travelling the globe researching and writing a series of books on urban culture and the complications of branding in a digital society.

He says the key to success is not technology but relevance:

'You can have the greatest social media technology or intranet structure in the world but, if the stuff you put on it isn't relevant to your audience, no-one will use it.'

Adz says that the challenges facing brands on the inside are the same as they are on the outside – employees are becoming more discerning and more demanding in the same way that consumers are – and you have to tackle those challenges the same way.

'Communication today is not about 'send' – it's about 'receive',' he says. 'If you want to engage consumers, you have to be prepared to get involved in their lives, so you can really understand where the opportunities are to improve things.'

It's the same on the inside. Managers need to understand what's going on in the lives of their employees and work out how to be relevant to them. If you don't start with that understanding, everything you communicate is just noise.

The rumour mill

Most of the communication that goes on inside an organisation (and pretty much all of the most interesting communication) is peer-to-peer.

It used to happen in conversations around the watercooler or the coffee machine. Now it's much more likely to happen in online exchanges on snapchat or instagram.

Businesses are usually wary of this kind of informal communication, because they can't control it. But the truth is that it plays a vital role in the way any organisation communicates.

It allows people to talk as one human being to another and it allows them to do it with people they trust. Two elements that are often conspicuously lacking in an organisation's more formal communication.

As a result, it helps people to form opinions of their own and make sense of things that are happening in their workplace.

In my experience, one of the best benchmarks of the health of a business is the way these informal conversations take place. If they're conducted furtively, in hushed voices, out in the car park or away from colleagues, that's a very bad sign. It means people are scared: they aren't sure who to trust; they're worried about being seen as a trouble-maker; they're not sure what it is or isn't okay to say.

If, on the other hand, they're conducted loudly and cheerily across the staff canteen – or if people are openly questioning what something means or why it's the right thing to do – that's a pretty healthy sign. People aren't scared: they just want to understand things better.

In both cases, all that's happening is that there's a vacuum of information and your employees are filling it. It's a human instinct: we like to be able to make sense of things. That's why we're always looking for meaning. And why, if you don't provide a real and understandable meaning, people will make one up for themselves (which is where conspiracy theories start).

Trying to 'quell rumours' is completely missing the point. So is trying to infiltrate the informal communication by setting up your own social media platform. If you don't want people to make up their own version of events, you need to make sure there isn't a vacuum.

Above all, you need to communicate with them in a way that

makes them feel involved and respected.

Make your audience the hero

About ten years ago, my colleague Nicky Flook was approached by a client who had a problem with customer service. Complaints were rising fast, there were service horror stories everywhere, and the chief executive had been grilled twice in three months on the BBC's consumer programme, *Watchdog*. What could she do to help them turn it around?

Nicky did a little digging and quickly realised the real problem was a cultural one. The people in their business weren't giving bad service because they were bad people: it was because they weren't tuned in to the idea of giving good service. All their targets were about completing tasks. They even seemed to take a grisly delight in their appalling reputation: at planning meetings, managers would vie to outdo each other with the worst customer service story from their store.

So Nicky set up a campaign that was all about highlighting the good stories instead. She ran a prize draw for the chance to win the trip of a lifetime to China. But instead of setting it up so it would reward the 'usual suspects' – the engaged individuals who always won prizes for service – she opened it up so everybody had a chance to win.

To be entered into the draw, you didn't have to do anything extraordinary. All you had to do was be nominated once for giving great service. Even the most disengaged people thought 'hey – I can do that.'

Take-up was about five times more than expected: over 40,000 nominations in the first three weeks. Soon, nobody was talking about the bad stories any more: they were vying to outdo each other with stories they were proud of instead.

Within six months, complaints were down by 18%, customer compliment letters were up by 39%. And the whole service culture shifted: in the process of giving great customer service once, people had discovered that it actually felt pretty good – so they kept on doing it.

It was a lovely campaign, which won a load of awards. But the real reason it worked is because it gave everyone a chance to be the hero of the story.

Get people involved

One business that has always known the value of involvement is the UK-based John Lewis Partnership, which was founded by store owner and philanthropist Spedan Lewis back in 1929.

He wanted to set up a business model that would feel fairer and more engaging, so he transferred his family's ownership of two

London department stores into a partnership made up of all the people who worked in them.

The Partnership's aims were set out in an ambitious set of Principles, of which the most important is Principle One. This describes the overall aim of the Partnership as being *'the happiness of all its members through their worthwhile and satisfying employment in a successful business.'*

It's a remarkable mission statement – the only other major public organisations with 'happiness' as an explicit aim are the United States and the Kingdom of Bhutan – and it has guided every decision the Partnership has made for the last 85 years.

Perhaps the most remarkable thing about it is that it doesn't mention customers at all. And yet the Partnership's branches consistently top surveys to find the best customer service in Britain.

In other words, focusing on the happiness of the people who work in it has made the Partnership a much better place for customers to shop (and, hence, a more successful business) than its more conventional rivals.

Mark Price – now Lord Price – is the UK's Minister of State for Trade & Investment. Before that, he spent 34 years in the John Lewis Partnership, working his way up from graduate trainee to Managing Director of its grocery business.

He says there's really no great secret to the Partnership's success:

'The only trick is in making sure the people who come in contact with your customers instinctively know the right thing to do – and feel empowered to do it. That's where the important decisions happen, all day, every day.'

In a nutshell...

#2 It's not about you. It's about them

You can't talk to people who aren't listening. Before you even worry about the content of your communication, you need to make sure your audience will want to engage with it – which means you need to make it feel relevant and interesting to them.

DO...

...start every piece of communication by thinking about the audience: who they are, what's going on in their lives and why they should care about what you want them to know.

DON'T...

...just transmit. You need to get people involved and give them the chance to feel like an active participant in the story.

Secret #3:
Know Yourself

Imagine your business is a bottle of wine.

If you ask a brand expert how to make it special, they'll talk to you about the way it's presented: the label, the shape of the bottle, the shelf-presence, the price architecture.

But if you ask a wine expert what makes a wine special, they'll answer with a single word: *terroir.*

It's a French word with no direct English equivalent, but which is sometimes translated as *'sense of place'*. Essentially, it's a distillation of all the characteristics – geography, climate, soil, drainage, exposure to wind and sun – that work together to give a wine its unique identity. It's why you can grow vines from exactly the same grape seeds in exactly the same way in two separate vineyards and the wines they make will taste totally different.

Organisations work in a similar way. You can take people with the same skills, backgrounds and characteristics, put them in two companies of the same size and type – and the products, service and customer experience that come out at the other end will be totally different.

The difference – the *terroir* – is what you and I might refer to as 'organisational culture.' And it's a big mistake to underestimate it, because it's what defines you as a business. (In fact, to my mind, it's a much more meaningful definition of 'brand' than the narrow way in which that word is usually applied. An appealing label or distinctive shape may help you sell the bottle once – but your long-term success depends on what happens after the cork comes out).

Some companies have a very strong and positive culture. This makes it easier for the people who work in those companies to know what the right thing is to do – and it makes them feel happier about where they work. Which, in turn, tends to make them more productive and to result in their customers having a better experience.

Not many companies are that fortunate, though. Most, if they're honest, would recognise that they have shortcomings in their culture. Their people don't instinctively know what the right thing is to do and don't always feel particularly happy to work there. They struggle to attract and keep good people – and to motivate them when they've got them.

So it's probably not surprising that, over the last 20 years, a large industry has emerged whose primary purpose is to help companies change their culture.

The results, in most cases, are fairly disappointing.

A little while ago, I was shopping in my local supermarket. On the shopping trolley, just below the handle, was this notice:

OUR VALUES ARE WHAT MAKE US DIFFERENT

I thought this was an interesting claim. Most companies have values, but they don't very often mention them to customers (presumably for fear of being held to account). So, when I got home, I decided to do an experiment.

I looked up this particular company's values on their website. There were five of them:

    1. Best for food and health

    2. Sourcing with integrity

    3. Respect for our environment

    4. Making a positive difference to our community

    5. A great place to work

All worthy values but, at first glance, they didn't seem strikingly 'different'.

So I looked up the values of every other company in the FTSE 100 and fed the results into a word cloud to see which words cropped up most often.

You'll find it on the next page.

Of course, it's not really surprising that so many companies have similar values. What company wouldn't want to be associated with characteristics like integrity and respect and teamwork? What company wouldn't want its employees to say it was a great place to work?

The problem is: if every company has values that sound broadly the same as every other company, don't those values become meaningless?

And, if your values are meaningless, how can you expect to build a strong and positive culture – one where your employees instinctively know what the right decision is? One where prospective employees instinctively know that yours is the business they want to be part of?

The answer is: you can't.

Here's a little exercise – just for fun...

Try to guess which major American business launched these values to its employees in July 2000.

(Answer on the next page. No peeking until you've guessed...)

Respect
We treat others as we would like to be treated ourselves. We do not tolerate abusive or disrespectful treatment. Ruthlessness, callousness and arrogance don't belong here.

Integrity
We work with customers and prospects openly, honestly and sincerely. When we say we will do something, we do it; when we say we cannot or will not do something, then we won't do it.

Communication
We have an obligation to communicate. Here, we take the time to talk with one another…and to listen. We believe that information is meant to move and that information moves people.

Excellence
We are satisfied with nothing less than the very best in everything we do. We will continue to raise the bar for everyone. The great fun here will be for all of us to discover just how good we can really be.

You probably noticed that the values sound pretty familiar. You could have pulled the headings straight out of the word cloud on the previous page. And they're so generic that you could apply them to any business in any market sector without changing a word.

As it happens, these particular values belonged to former US energy giant Enron. They appeared as part of a 64-page code of ethics sent out to Enron's employees, with this stirring introduction from Chairman Kenneth Lay:

'We want to be proud of Enron and to know that it enjoys a reputation for fairness and honesty and that it is respected... Enron's reputation finally depends on its people, on you and me. Let's keep that reputation high.'

I won't go into all 64 pages (even allowing for the irony value, it's not a gripping read – if you're interested, it's all online).

What *is* interesting is that, at the same time they were publishing this vast ethical bible to their 20,000 employees, Enron's leaders were committing indictable offences on a spectacular scale: dozens of counts of money laundering, insider trading, securities fraud.

18 months after the code of ethics was published, Enron filed for bankruptcy. A number of senior executives (including Kenneth Lay and CEO Jeff Skilling) were sent to jail.

Is it really surprising that people are wary when companies make bombastic pronouncements about their values?

Culture has to be authentic – you can't fake it

Just out of mischievousness, I took my earlier values word cloud and made an 'anti-values' version of it, by replacing the words with their nearest opposites. This is what it looked like:

The reason I did this was because I thought it would help to highlight the pointlessness of the original value statements. If the alternatives to your values are so obviously bad things, why do you need to mention them as values in the first place? Surely, they should be a given?

When I tested this hypothesis with an audience drawn from some of the same FTSE100 companies that I'd used for my values sample, it had an interesting effect.

I started by putting up the first word cloud, and there were a few knowing nods and wry smiles. But the truth is that this wasn't a revelation to the audience. Most of them had worked in two or more large businesses and they'd already worked out for themselves that everybody's values were basically the same.

It was when I put up the second, negative word cloud that the audience became really animated. Partly because they found it funny – and partly because they found it much easier to relate the negative characteristics to their business than the positive ones.

One of the delegates stood up and jabbed his finger, excitedly: 'Now *that s*ounds like my company.' Everyone laughed, because he'd said what most of them were thinking.

You only have to listen to conversations in the car park or canteen of any large organisation to realise that, in many cases, the image that organisation wishes to project is one the majority of its employees simply don't recognise.

That may have been good enough 20 years ago, but it's not good enough now. Philip Davies is the European President for brand consultancy Siegel & Gale. He says that behaving in a more human and authentic way is becoming an increasingly critical factor in business success:

'The organisations that do well now are generally the ones that know they're about more than just making money. When you look at technology companies, they're getting closer to that. When you look at banks, they're probably furthest away.'

That's not a recent phenomenon. For some time now, banks have been a stark example of how wide the gap can be between what you promise in your advertising and what your customers experience.

But it seems that even banks are, finally, starting to get the message...

The bank that feels human

EPSI is a European body which tracks the customer satisfaction ratings of businesses in the banking and utility sectors. Its 2016 survey shows a steady pattern of improvement among customer satisfaction scores for the UK's leading consumer banks –up around the 75% mark on average, compared to the sub-70% levels they'd been running at four years earlier.

However, they're all still nowhere near the 84% satisfaction level which Handelsbanken has consistently enjoyed over the past ten years.

Handelsbanken was founded in Stockholm in 1871. It grew steadily, if unspectacularly, for the next hundred years. And then, in 1970, it made an interesting decision.

Just as other banks (especially in the UK) began looking for ways to consolidate and become more centralised, Handelsbanken went in exactly the opposite direction.

The bank's then head, Jan Wallander, established a philosophy of decentralisation and local empowerment – 'The Branch *is* the Bank' – which still guides Handelsbanken today. The emphasis of this approach is firmly on local relationships: branches making good decisions based on their personal knowledge of customers. Quality is prized over quantity. There are no sales targets: it's not the volume of business that matters, but the value over the long-term.

That long-term view is reflected in the way Handelsbanken rewards its employees. It eschews the traditional annual bonus in favour of a healthy basic salary and a unique profit-sharing scheme. The bank's target is to beat the average profitability rate of other listed banks: any profit above that figure is placed into a fund distributed fairly among all employees. However, you only receive your share when you turn 60 – one reason why employee retention is so high.

The other reason is simple: emotional engagement. Employees feel connected to the philosophy of Handelsbanken in a way that seems far removed from the rest of the financial services industry.

The bank's UK head, Anders Bouvin, says that working in the branch network was the best thing he ever did: 'I flourished building customer relationships – there's nothing better than being empowered to make customers satisfied.'

The result is that Handelsbanken has continued to grow slowly, but steadily. It now has a presence in 25 countries, including 207 branches across the UK.

In every year since 1972, it has achieved higher profitability than the average for other listed banks. It also enjoys a much lower loan loss ratio than its competitors, coming through the recent financial crisis with an enviably strong balance sheet – prompting one city commentator to describe the bank as 'thrillingly boring'.

Perhaps most tellingly, Handelsbanken's customer satisfaction scores are head and shoulders above its rivals. In Sweden, it has been top of the customer satisfaction rankings ever since surveys first started in 1989. In the UK, its customer satisfaction level is nearly ten percentage points better than its nearest rival – and its customer loyalty nearly 15 points better.

That's what an authentic culture can do for you.

Think Different

A lot of companies already think they know what their *terroir* is, because they've spent a lot of time and trouble developing a mission statement (or 'purpose' or 'vision').

The problem is that most of these statements are neither credible nor emotionally-compelling.

There are some honourable exceptions. I like Google's – 'to organise the world's information and make it universally accessible and useful.' And Ben and Jerry's – 'we make the best possible ice cream in the best possible way.' My favourite always used to be toy manufacturer Tomy – 'to make children happy' – but I looked on their website recently and they've changed it to something far duller.

The ones that work tend to be expressed in human terms. They're simple and short. They combine a ring of truth with a glimpse of personality: not just 'what we do' but 'why it matters' and 'who we are'.

Very few mission statements pull this off successfully, though. Most are a laboured compromise: a list of functional agenda items horse-traded in committee until any shred of personality has been beaten out of them, then topped off with a few consultancy clichés, such as 'excellence' and 'deliver'.

Dell, for example, defines its mission as wanting to be 'the most successful IT systems company in the world by delivering the best customer experience in all markets we serve.' It backs this up with a list of seven characteristics ('highest quality', 'competitive pricing', 'superior corporate citizenship') that are so obvious and dull you can guess what they are without me writing the list in full.

The point is that it's generic: there's nothing distinctive or human or engaging in it. There are 61 words and you could apply every single one of them to Hewlett Packard or IBM or Acer and no-one would even notice. Which may, perhaps, explain why Dell doesn't really stand out from the mass of other technology companies.

The obvious contrast is with Apple (although I use the example with caution, because it's been used so often that there's a risk of it becoming meaningless dogma).

When Steve Jobs came back to Apple in 1997, the company he'd founded was drifting into becoming a 'me-too' manufacturer.

Jobs immediately set about streamlining the business. He axed around 70% of Apple's existing product lines and shut down 'OpenDoc' – the ambitious flexible software platform, which many analysts had identified as a nerdy white elephant that would bleed Apple dry.

Jobs re-focused the business on consumer needs – and

relaunched it under the banner of 'think different'. This prompted one of the most iconic and successful advertising campaigns of all time. More importantly, it also provided a very clear sense of what Apple should stand for.

This was not universally popular with Apple employees.

There's a fascinating video on youtube, which shows a Q&A session hosted by Jobs for Apple developers in the early days of his return. He gets some very hostile questions and he handles them brilliantly – by being straight and explaining his strategy so clearly and compellingly that everyone gets it.

'You've got to start with the customer experience', he says at one point, 'and work backwards from there to the technology. You can't start with the technology and figure out how you're going to sell it.'

That may seem obvious to us today but, in Microsoft-dominated 1997, the idea of consumer experience trumping technological know-how was close to heresy.

Jobs's performance at that Q&A session is an absolute masterclass in how to manage and communicate change. Whatever you may think of him, there's no question that 'think different' – and his focus on developing consumer-pleasing products – was what transformed Apple into the giant it is today.

You have to know what you really stand for

Another business closely identified with its founder is Virgin. The Group's mission statement – *'Be different by being better'* – is a reasonable summary of its approach to the market. But it barely scratches the surface of what Virgin is really all about: rebellion, mischievousness, daring, fun, plain-speaking, common sense, consumer-championing, charm.

Luckily, no-one who works for Virgin needs to have these characteristics spelt out for them, because they've got Richard Branson as a living, breathing example of them. The same was true of Steve Jobs at Apple, or Anita Roddick at Body Shop. It's a little like the 'What would Jesus do?' bumper stickers you see in the American midwest: if you want to know what the right thing is to do, just imagine the boss and what they'd do in your place.

The problem is: what happens when the boss changes?

Is Body Shop the same business without Roddick? Is Apple the same business without Jobs? Would Virgin be the same business without Branson? The answer in all three cases, I suspect, is no. And that carries a risk.

When the purpose, direction and values of an organisation are very closely identified with one individual, the removal of that individual may end up making all those things seem less clear to the people who work in it.

So just imagine how much bigger that risk must be in a business where the leadership keeps changing.

Every time a new CEO comes into a large business, they're under pressure to put their stamp on it. This is especially true in countries like the US and UK, where Chief Executives get paid eye-watering salaries and shareholders expect to see a return on that investment.

The problem is that 'putting your stamp on it' usually means tearing up what the previous incumbent did and taking the business in a new direction. This is quite exciting when you're close to it: new departments are set up in the head office, dead wood is cut away, you hear words like 'transformation', 'pace' and 'momentum'. There's a stimulating debate about who you are as a business and what you stand for. It feels like something big is happening.

But, if you're one of the people working at the customer end of the business – the shop-floor, the call centre, the delivery network – you may have a slightly different view, as the business swings from one direction to the next and then (three years later, when the firebrand CEO has moved on and been replaced by another) back again.

Real purpose goes a lot deeper than commercial strategy – and a lot deeper than words. If you try to define it with a mission statement, or values, or (God help me) 'pillars', you're missing the point. You can polish those words all you like: they won't help people make better decisions.

Real purpose is a sense of self, a corporate *terroir.* If you aren't blessed with a charismatic figurehead who embodies it and sticks around for the long term, you have to find some other way of capturing it and bringing it to life.

And that starts with the people you bring in to your business.

In a nutshell...

#3 Know yourself

Culture is hugely important in bringing your brand to life. Most organisations struggle to develop a clear and positive culture, because they're trying to articulate it with generic value statements and an uninspiring purpose. You can't fake it. The businesses that succeed are increasingly the ones that can define themselves in a clear and meaningful way.

DO...

...work hard at explaining your business in a way that will give your people a clear sense of identity – and a guide to help them know what the right thing is to do.

DON'T...

...fall into the trap of choosing values because they sound 'worthy'. If they sound like everybody else's values – or if they don't resonate with the people in your business – they'll just be ignored.

Secret #4:
Start with the right people

When Ernest Shackleton was looking for a team to accompany him on his 1912 Antarctic expedition, he ran this ad in the *Times:*

It's a perfect example of the copywriter's art: short, to the point, authentic – and pitched perfectly to appeal to the target audience.

Most of us would read these words and think 'you'd have to be insane to get involved in that'. But a very small number of people – perhaps two or three in a million – would read them with a soaring heart and think 'my God, this is just the opportunity I've been waiting for.' Those two or three were exactly who Shackleton wanted.

A lot of business leaders have the experience of trying to make people do something they don't want to do. Shackleton didn't have that problem. In fact, his biggest problem was usually trying to stop his team doing something selfless and heroic that was likely to lead to their unnecessary and dramatic death.

Like all great communicators, he'd found a way to connect directly with the right people.

Now, contrast Shackleton's ad with a typical recruitment ad. What would you expect to find? A bit of trumpet-blowing ('we are the largest manufacturer of widgets in Europe')? Some generic flattery ('you are a self-motivated go-getter with a strong track record of success')? A few logistical carrots ('highly competitive benefits package')?

There's nothing specifically wrong with any of that. It's just that it's purely transactional. There's no charm or engagement: you're not appealing to a higher motivation. You're just talking about swapping money for skills – and that's how you're framing the context for any future working relationship. Before they've even joined you.

Find people who believe what you believe

The biggest difference between communicating on the inside of a business and communicating on the outside is that, with internal communication, you get to choose your audience.

These are not faceless consumers that you hope will buy your products. These are people you invited to the party. At some point, you, or one of your colleagues, had a face-to-face conversation with every one of them and made a conscious decision to offer them a job.

And yet, statistically, it's likely that well over half of them don't particularly want to be there – and don't feel engaged with the work they're doing. That can damage even the strongest brand.

Body Shop was one of the most successful retail stories of the 1980's: they had a very strong sense of identity and meaning that resonated powerfully with customers. The business grew by an average of 50% every year and the share price went up so fast it was known as the 'stock that defies gravity'.

But, when Body Shop first expanded into North America, the business fell flat on its face.

Founder Anita Roddick later acknowledged that the biggest factor in the failure was hiring people with the wrong values and attitude:

'We didn't know how to look for signals of bullying, the signals of verbal violence, the signals of indifference to our reputation or mediocrity. We didn't even know how to detect indifference to retailing.'

In other words: the problem was not that the people they hired couldn't do the job. They could. They just didn't care *how* they did it.

It's a lot easier to get the people in your organisation to behave the right way if you only hire the right people to start with. Which is why it's peculiar how little care many companies appear to put into the hiring process.

Shaun McIlrath is the creative director of Iris, the UK's largest independent advertising agency and a man who has seen more than his fair share of misguided attempts at recruitment.

'Companies struggle to process the idea that they need to sell themselves to potential recruits,' he says. 'Especially big companies. They've got loads of applicants for every job, so they think the hard part is whittling it down to people with the right skills. But that's actually quite easy: you can train people to do almost anything. The hard part is finding people who will make good decisions because they instinctively understand what the right thing is to do.'

In his excellent book *Brand Authenticity*, Australian academic Michael Beverland tells the story of a Southwest Airlines selection process.

The airline was recruiting pilots: they invited applicants to an aircraft hangar. It was a hot day, there was no air conditioning and the pilots all turned up in dark suits.

The Airline offered shorts to help the applicants feel more comfortable. Some accepted gratefully; others (no doubt anxious to preserve their dignity) declined.

Only the pilots who accepted the shorts were offered a job. It was a test: they could all do the job, but Southwest Airlines wanted more than that. They wanted pilots who would be willing to ignore protocol in favour of common sense.

They wanted to make sure they'd be starting with the right people.

Make it feel special

One of the defining characteristics of any high performing team – whether in sport, in the military, in academia or in business – is that the people in that team feel they're part of something special. They're proud to have earned their place; proud to pull on the jersey or wear the badge.

Which is why it always strikes me as odd when organisations that aspire to be high-performing don't put much care into the way they attract and hire their new recruits.

It's often a very mechanistic process. Over 71% of applications for jobs in the U.S. are never seen by a human being at all: the initial short-listing is done by a computer algorithm.

Even if you do get past the machine, the human element may not be much better. The imperative to 'keep headcount down' tends to mean that recruitment only happens in response to an urgent need: a busy manager who needs to get someone in to fill a gap and relieve pressure. They're not really interested in culture or personality: all they want to know is 'can you do the job?' Which, let's be honest, doesn't feel that special.

Luckily, there are some organisations that do get it right.

Zappos – the US-based internet shoe company – is a business that set out to be famous for service and has designed its recruitment process accordingly.

There are two separate interviews for every new hire: a skills interview and a culture interview. Candidates have to pass both before they're offered a job.

Even then, there's one final test: would-be recruits who've made it this far are offered $2000 *not* to take the job. On the face of it, this sounds bonkers, but it actually makes perfect sense.

Why? Because $2000 is an appreciable sum of money. If you're at all unsure about the job, the smart thing would be to pocket the money, leave and treat yourself to a nice holiday on Zappos. It makes the decision easy.

It also works out a lot better for Zappos than if they were to invest in your development, only to see you leave eight months down the line.

If, on the other hand, you decide to turn down the money and take the job, you've made a positive psychological choice to be at Zappos – which makes it far more likely that you'll embrace their culture and flourish in the long term.

Everything about it gives you an understanding of the Zappos personality – uncompromising, quirky, can do, smart.

And it means that everyone who joins Zappos knows that everyone else around them has made the same commitment they did. Which makes them feel part of something pretty special.

All you have to do from there is make sure they keep feeling it.

Induct as you mean to go on

Remember this diagram from the first section?

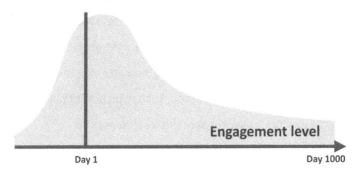

It's a reminder that most organisations – especially large ones – are depressingly efficient at taking motivated people and then de-motivating them.

It's easy to understand how this happens. It's like any new relationship: at the start, you only see the good things. Then, after a while, you start to take the good things for granted (or stop believing them) and, instead, you start to notice some less-good things. The day the less-good things outweigh the good things is the day your relationship is likely to be in trouble.

That's why you can never afford to stop selling your business to your employees.

If you truly believe that people are your most important asset, then you need to keep working hard at the relationship, so that the positives will always feel positive and the negatives are kept to a minimum. You need to remind them how they felt that first day they joined you.

Over the long term, this is about building and maintaining a sense of being part of something special. We touched on this just now in terms of how you attract the right people. Over the next few chapters, we'll be exploring how you maintain it over the course of their career with you, so that, instead of tailing off sharply over time, their engagement level stays high.

For now, let's consider how you bring people into your business: the brand induction, the employee manual, the way you introduce them to their team, the way they're treated by the people who are already there.

In many organisations, this can often feel like the first day at a new school. New starters are bombarded with information from lots of different sources. They feel self-conscious when they step into the canteen and have to figure out how the queue works. Or get introduced at their first morning meeting when they're not expecting it. Everything is strange and different and confusing. And none of it is explained by the rambling, daunting and legally-worded 100-page employee manual with which they're presented on their first day – and which will sit, unopened, in their desk drawer until the first time they have a contract query.

Happily, it doesn't always work that way.

When new employees join the US retailer Nordstrom, they're presented with their 'employee handbook', which is a small piece of card bearing the following 74 words:

Welcome to Nordstrom.

We're glad to have you with our Company.

Our number one goal is to provide outstanding customer

service.

Set both your personal and professional goals high.

We have great confidence in your ability to achieve them.

So our employee handbook is very simple.

We have only one rule:

Use good judgment in all situations.

Feel free to ask your department manager, store manager or personnel manager any question at any time.

It's an admirably clear sentiment – and, to anyone who's ever wrestled their way through the usual turgid employee handbook, pleasingly concise.

But that doesn't mean you'd be able to emulate Nordstrom's extraordinary reputation for customer care simply by coming up with something equally pithy.

The reason it works is because of the whole Nordstrom package that surrounds it, starting with the right people.

Nordstrom is famously picky about who it recruits, prizing 'niceness' above skills or qualifications. It then gives those nice employees three very important things:

1. a clear and single-minded goal ('to provide outstanding customer service')

2. the confidence to let their inherent niceness guide their decision-making ('use good judgment in all situations')

3. and the trust that their managers and colleagues will support them.

Clarity, confidence, trust. (Sound familiar?)

Perhaps the most important element, though, is what happens next. Nordstrom reinforces its service commitment by encouraging people to share and celebrate stories of employees who exemplify it. It's a great way of making the same point over and over again – and making it feel fresh and authentic every time.

That's why no-one who works for Nordstrom is in any doubt about what the right thing is to do in any situation.

And why, if you want your brand to enjoy a reputation like theirs, you need to start by having a clear and consistent story.

In a nutshell...

#4 Start with the right people

It's much easier to engage people when they believe in the same things you do. The way you recruit employees and bring them into your business will make an enormous difference to your customers' experience.

DO...

...set out to create a relationship with your employees that's based on human characteristics and values, rather than a purely transactional one.

DON'T...

...be complacent. Once you've found the right people, you need to keep working hard to remind them why they should feel good to be part of your organisation.

Secret #5:
Have a good story (and stick to it)

Human beings are wired to look for meaning: it's one of our most basic instincts.

If you spend time with the aboriginal tribes in Australia, you'll hear spoken histories that date back thousands of years, passed on word-for-word from one generation to the next.

Before telescopes and space probes helped us understand what stars really are, goatherds in ancient Greece used to look up at the night sky and tell stories about the shapes they found in it: Perseus, Andromeda, Orion.

Stories like these were a way for our ancestors to make sense of the world around them – and stories are still an important way for us to make sense of the complexity that surrounds us in our daily and working lives.

They help us translate abstract ideas into tangible examples. They allow us to articulate and define the things that matter to us. And they build a sense of shared identity: they help us remember which tribe we belong to.

Unfortunately, the idea of story-telling has been hijacked in recent years. Stories are now peddled as a technique for investing dull strategies with ersatz drama ('Share the journey of our new stock management system...'). Businesses are awash with stories: they've become just another communication fad.

Which is a shame, because that's totally missing the point.

Engaging people with your business is all about emotion and belief. That's why the organisations that succeed tend to be the ones that have a clear sense of who they are and what they stand for. If you get it right, it makes it easy for you to attract and motivate people who believe in what you believe in.

So the trick is not to keep making up different stories for every little change you want to make.

The trick is to have a single, consistent narrative that helps people know what the right thing is to do.

Start with 'why'

Simon Sinek is an American ethnographer and leadership expert.

In 2009, he wrote a best-selling book called 'Start with why'. He also gave an online TED talk based on it, which became the second most viewed TED talk of all time. So you may well be familiar with his ideas already – but, in case you're not, let me give you a very quick recap.

Sinek uses a simple device, which he calls the 'golden circle', to explain how some businesses are able to engage much more powerfully than others with consumers and employees.

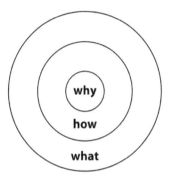

The outer ring of the circle is 'what we do'.

The middle ring is 'how we do it'.

And the central ring is 'why we do it' – what's our purpose (other than the obvious one of making money)?

Most businesses define themselves in terms of 'what', because that feels like the easiest and most concrete thing. But Sinek says the businesses that succeed best are the ones that are able to define themselves in terms of 'why'.

This is all down to the way our brain makes decisions. The part of our brain that controls decision-making – the limbic brain – is the same part of our brain that deals with emotions. But it's not the part of the brain that deals with language: that happens in our 'higher', human brain.

In other words, our decision-making is much more closely influenced by what we feel than by what we rationally understand. This is why you often hear people justify overruling rational evidence on the grounds that 'it just doesn't feel right'.

Although Sinek's thesis is primarily about engaging customers, it's every bit as important on the inside of your business.

The point is that we rely on instinct and emotion to tell us what the right thing is to do. That's how your customers make decisions ('do I like what they stand for?'). It's also how your employees make decisions ('do I know what the right thing is to do?').

The problem, in both cases, comes when we make those decisions less clear.

If you took the time to analyse all the communication going on inside your business, you'd probably find that most of it falls into the category of 'how' ('our plan / your role').

That's fine if your business is simple and you only need people to follow a process. But, the more complex your business gets, the harder it is for you to be prescriptive about 'how': you need your employees to be able to make decisions for themselves.

Which means they need to have an instinctive understanding of what the right thing is to do.

Focus on what makes you *you*

Sinek's theories struck a powerful chord. Since 'start with why' first appeared, organisations all over the world have been trying to reinvigorate themselves with a meaningful purpose that will engage their customers and staff.

Most have failed to pull it off convincingly. Which is hardly surprising: it's a lot easier to come up with a meaningful story when you're starting your business than it is to reinvent a culture that's evolved over many years.

But it is possible. Steve Jobs did it with Apple. BMW did it with Mini.

One of my favourite examples is Lego, a brand I remember fondly from my childhood. Lego lost its way a little in the 1990s: competition from 'me-too' rivals was hurting margins in its core plastic brick market. The company responded with a flurry of random brand extensions – clothes, watches, a TV show – that confused customers, delivered a patchy experience and did nothing to improve profitability.

In 2000, Lego found itself on the verge of bankruptcy and the management team decided to go 'back to the brick': focusing on core products and a much simpler brand message.

Instead of expanding into markets they weren't familiar with, they built highly successful partnerships with other brands that would add value to their core ranges: 'Lego Star Wars', for instance.

And, when they did venture into different markets, they did it with people who were leaders in those markets: the Legoland theme parks are owned and operated by Merlin Entertainments; the two hugely successful Lego movies were made by Warner Brothers.

Instead of diluting the Lego brand (as their earlier extensions had done), these new activities have spectacularly reinforced it. Over the past decade, Lego has climbed steadily up Interbrand's annual register of brand value: in 2017, it leapfrogged Disney, Apple and Coca-Cola to be named the world's most valuable brand.

According to Jorgen Vig Knudstorp, the CEO who has led the business since 2004 and is widely credited with its revival, the key has been to reconnect with what really makes Lego unique.

'Most companies don't die from starvation – they die from indigestion. Where we went wrong in the past is that, instead of trying a new extension once every three to five years, we were building three to five extensions every year. People lose focus on the core business as they pursue these sexy new ideas. For me, the shift has been to focus on the core as the most exciting thing we do, because that is what makes us different.'

This simple insight has helped the business and its customers to reconnect with the values that built the Lego brand in the first place: creativity, quality and play.

To celebrate its 80th birthday, Lego made an animated corporate film that tells the story of its evolution from a carpenter's workshop to one of the world's most popular toys. At 17 minutes, you might think it's a little indulgent. But it's well-made, charming and – most importantly – it reinforces Lego's product difference and values.

It feels like a family video, in much the same way that the Lego brand feels like a natural part of most homes. Lego is likeable – and, as the Interbrand ranking would attest, that's about as close as you can get to a one-word definition of a great brand.

What makes a good brand story?

There's no single template for a great brand story: they come in every shape and size. But all of them are about the same thing: finding a meaningful way to differentiate yourself.

Many brands have a historical 'founder myth' and this can be quite a useful shorthand (depending on the founder), but it's very far from essential. The recent trend for trawling through the archives, to find some individual to reinvent as a personification of what you stand for, can often be counterproductive. For every golden-hearted philanthropist, you'll find a rapacious exploiter: trying to spin them into a colourful hero is only likely to draw attention to the less savoury reality (imagine if Volkswagen had to market itself as 'the car Hitler dreamed of' – true, but toxic).

I think there are five big themes that shape most brand stories and, although it's a little artificial to shoehorn everything into these groups, it gives you a reasonable starting-point:

>**1. Social meaning** *('a better way')*. One obvious example in this group is the John Lewis Partnership, which is owned by its employees and whose founder, Spedan Lewis, saw it as a 'practical alternative to communism'. Other examples are Body Shop or the Co-op – although both have endured a tailing-off in their fortunes as they have moved further away from the values that gave them meaning.
>
>**2. Rebellion** *('a better attitude')*. Disruptive brands, like Virgin and Innocent, have grown by entering markets dominated by unloved giants and positioning themselves as a more authentic and relatable alternative: a plucky David to their lumbering Goliath. It can be difficult to keep pulling this trick off as you get larger – especially if (as in the case of US drinks brand Snapple) you get snapped up by one of the Goliath brands you were originally set up to

oppose.

3. Invention *('a better idea')*. Creativity is always a compelling story: it's helped to build engineering brands like Dyson and Otis, restaurants like El Bulli and any number of fashion brands. But what happens if you're perceived to lose that creative edge? In 1990, one of my clients was Compaq, the US PC maker. At the time, Compaq was a massive success story: the fastest-growing start-up in US corporate history, built on the brand promise of 'it simply works better'. The trouble was that everyone else caught them up: in 2002, they were bought by rival HP and, in 2012, the Compaq name vanished altogether.

4. Quality *('a better product')*. Volkswagen could hardly have had a less auspicious start to its existence, but its corporate narrative of reliability has been earned over time – and has proved solid enough to survive the reputational iceberg of cheating US emissions tests. That same sense of reliability applies to safety. If a British Airways flight crash-lands, people will still feel confident about getting on the next one. Would they feel as confident about Ryanair?

5. People *('a better service')*. This final category is perhaps the most interesting, because it doesn't require you to have anything special in your brand history or product set-up. No unique founder, or purpose, or technology, or attitude: just a willingness to bend over backwards for your customers. Avis built a global brand on 'we try harder' and US retailer Nordstrom has become a global benchmark for service (we'll talk more about them in a moment). You have to keep trying, of course: when your story is about service, you really are only as good as the last customer experience.

Beyond these broad story-lines, there are a number of other characteristics that are common to most compelling brand narratives. We'll talk about these in more detail over the following chapters, but there are three key elements it's worth highlighting now:

Make it single-minded. The more things you give people to think about, the harder they'll find it to know what the right thing is to do.

Make it emotional. The human brain finds it a lot easier to remember things when they prompt an emotional response. A strong feeling of excitement, or pleasure, or humour, or sadness, releases dopamine into your brain – and this acts like a kind of mental post-it note, making it easy for your sub-conscious to access that memory.

Make it relatable. Remember: it's not about you – it's about them. Your audience is much more likely to be engaged by a story they can feel part of.

Involve your audience

I spent the early part of my life in Nigeria, which has a rich tradition of story-telling – especially among the Hausa tribes of Northern Nigeria, who like to share 'dilemma tales' around the evening meal.

These are stories where no specific ending is provided. Instead, the audience is given a set of facts and then a number of possible outcomes, and invited to share their own opinions about what should happen next.

For example, in one story, a young man is treated badly by his cruel father, so he runs away. He is taken in by the kindly chief of a neighbouring village, who adopts him as his son and treats him well. But then, through a peculiar combination of circumstances, the real father and adoptive father find themselves pitted against one another. The boy is forced to choose which of them may live and which must die. Where should his loyalty lie?

The stories serve a double purpose: as entertainment and as a kind of moral litmus test – a way to debate and establish social norms. They engage the audience by getting them involved.

In the last chapter, we touched on the American department store Nordstrom and how it has built a reputation for extraordinary customer service by encouraging customers and employees (known as 'Nordies') to share stories about their experiences.

These stories have become a part of US consumer culture. Customers delight in telling them. If you look online, you'll find dozens of different examples: the Nordie who drove six hundred miles to make sure a wedding hat got delivered; the Nordie who found a customer's bags in the car park, along with a flight itinerary, and raced to the airport to reunite the bags with the grateful customer just as she was boarding her flight.

Stories like this make Nordstrom employees feel like a breed apart. They're proud of the reputation their business enjoys, confident that they're surrounded by people who feel the same way – and eager to write their own chapter in the company's legend. These are classic characteristics of an elite team.

What's especially interesting is that there's no attempt to 'sanitise' stories about decisions that were good for the customer but bad for short-term profits (like the Nordie in

Alaska who refunded a customer $145 for a pair of snow tires – even though Nordstrom has never sold tires in its entire history). Nordstrom's leaders take a longer view: decisions like this may hit the bottom line in the short term, but the long term reputational gain of such uncompromising service is worth it.

No one who works at Nordstrom is in any doubt about what the company wants – and expects – to be famous for. Which makes it easy for them to know what the right thing is to do.

Consistency is the key to memory

Nordstrom's stories work so well because they all reinforce the same strong message: we are totally uncompromising about customer service.

Advertising (at least good advertising) works the same way. The lines you tend to remember – 'Just do it', 'We try harder', 'Should've gone to Specsavers' – don't come from one-off commercials. They're built up over long-running campaigns.

This is because repetition is the key to memory. The human brain is much more likely to remember something if (a) the initial memory is encoded in a stimulating way and (b) that memory is re-activated by a regular recreation of the same stimulus.

In other words, if you want to establish a clear sense of who you are and what you stand for, don't confuse people by constantly changing your story. All successful brands instinctively understand this – which is why, when advertisers come up with a winning strap-line, they don't change it.

And yet, on the inside, the story changes all the time: new purpose, new values, new priorities.

A lot of this is to do with pressure and numbers. The average tenure of a CEO in a FTSE100 company is six years. Their average salary in 2015 was £5.5million (nearly 200 times as much as an average worker in those companies). So it follows that anyone clambering into the CEO hot seat might reasonably expect to feel some pressure to perform. CEOs are much more visible – much more exposed to questioning by the media and shareholders – than they used to be. When you combine this with an energetic, alpha personality, it's not surprising that so many of them come bursting into a business and want to shake things up.

But, to the people working in those companies, 'shaking things up' often feels quite a lot less exciting than it does at the centre. Many people who've worked in the same business for a while have the sensation of going round in circles. They see the same ideas coming in and out of fashion, they hear the same logic applauded and then derided. Like minor functionaries in Stalin's

Soviet Union, they learn to keep their heads down, follow the new line and watch for signs that the wind is shifting again.

In other words, the exact opposite of the consistency and clarity that brands seek to create for their consumers.

If you want your brand to be consistent and clear on the outside, you have to start by making it consistent and clear on the inside.

In a nutshell...

#5 Have a good story (and stick to it)

Meaning is the key to motivation. If you want people to feel connected with your business, you need to reach them on an emotional level ('why') and not just a rational level ('what' and 'how').

DO...

...articulate what your business is about in a way that will make people want to be part of it.

DON'T...

...keep changing your story. You'll just confuse everyone.

Secret #6
Turn down the background noise

According to Boston Consulting Group, businesses today are 35 times more complicated on average than they were in 1955 (the year the Fortune 500 list was created).

In some ways, this is very good. It's what makes greater consumer choice and convenience possible. It's the reason why you can lie in bed in Croydon, browsing specialist car components from a dealer in Cincinnati, choose and buy one with a couple of taps of your finger and have it delivered to your front door next day.

But it also means that the business delivering your car components is a much more complex place to work than it used to be when its customers all lived within a ten-mile radius and walked in off the street.

A 2013 study in the Harvard Business Review showed that modern office workers tend to switch activities several hundred times a day: from phone to email to social media to meeting to research. When they compared productivity levels, it was clear (and unsurprising) that the more workers switched activities during the course of a day, the less productive they were. By contrast, those who were able to focus on one task for longer periods were dramatically more productive.

John Medina is a molecular biologist and director of the Brain Center for applied learning research at Seattle Pacific University. In 2008, he wrote a brilliant book called *Brain Rules,* which explains the key factors governing how our brains work (and which ought to be required reading for anyone who works in communication).

Among many other gems in the book, Medina explains why 'multi-tasking' is a neurological impossibility. Put simply: our brains are not able to pay attention to more than one thing at once. We may think we're performing several tasks in parallel, but we're actually performing them in a series. Every time we shift from one task to another, or back again, our brains go through the same sequence of firing up the neurons and accessing stored information that they go through when we first start the task. This is incredibly inefficient.

Every time one of your employees switches from a phone call to an email to a meeting to writing a report to planning for a conference call, they're wasting time and mental energy rebooting their brain between each task. With the result that they get less done over the course of a day – and what they do get done is done less well.

Medina's research shows that people who are interrupted take an average of 50% longer to complete a task and will make 50% more errors. You can't concentrate on two things at once.

That's why people who talk on mobile phones while driving – even when hands-free – are statistically far more likely to have an accident. When we're thinking about too many things, we get stressed and we make bad decisions.

Yet juggling tasks is a badge of corporate honour: the busier you are, the more you're seen to be contributing.

This is because we're still stuck in an outdated industrial model, where people are rewarded for their volume of output on the supposition that, the more you make, the more productive you're being.

Even if all you're really making is noise.

Cutting out the interruptions

If you ask most people in most businesses, they'll say the two biggest drains on their time are meetings and email.

In a Forbes magazine study, 85% of the executives interviewed said they were unhappy with the way meetings work in their business: too many of them, taking up too much time, for too little benefit. The Dutch even have a word for it: *vergaderziekte* – *'meeting sickness'.*

In recent years, US tech companies have led a conscious shift away from the traditional meeting culture.

Meetings at online retail giant Amazon begin with what CEO Jeff Bezos describes as 'study hall'. Instead of starting with a powerpoint presentation, the audience spends 30 minutes silently reading through a six-page narrative memo.

This does the same job as the slideshow, but with three important advantages:

> 1. It forces the presenter to write their ideas out in complete sentences rather than bullet points – which encourages greater clarity (and more careful thought on their part about how they express an idea)
>
> 2. It avoids interruptions: the meeting doesn't start until everyone has read through to the end of the memo (which may often answer a question they would otherwise have raised earlier)
>
> 3. It means the presenter can be certain everyone in the room has given the idea their full attention (which would probably not be the case if you sent it out as a pre-read).

At the same time, many businesses have been looking for ways to cut down the amount of time spent dealing with correspondence through email and other electronic messaging.

The French company ATOS made headlines when it announced that it was turning off email in a bid to make its employees more productive. Other companies have followed suit – although they often simply substitute another form of communication: instant messaging or social media.

More recently, German carmaker Daimler announced that any emails sent to its employees while they were on holiday would be automatically deleted.

'Our employees should relax on holiday and not read work-related emails,' explained their HR Director. 'This way, they can start back after the holidays with a clean desk and no traffic jam in their in-tray. That's an emotional relief.'

Of course, examples like this are only noteworthy because they're still comparatively rare.

Conflicting priorities, complex tasks and a quagmire of information are a normal and accepted part of most working lives. It's difficult just to switch them off.

But what you *can* do is encourage habits and disciplines that will limit the damage from this constant juggling.

For instance, you can restrict the times when people read and send email (so they don't feel under constant pressure to check their devices, especially outside the office).

You can set guidelines for social media activity.

You can encourage a wider culture of succinctness, where people are rewarded for summarising key points and penalised for including too much unnecessary detail.

What you should be very careful about, however, is just turning information streams off.

Don't communicate less – communicate better

There's a myth that the best way to cut out noise is to stop communicating.

'Our employees don't want more information,' you often hear senior managers say when explaining why they're shutting down a communication channel. 'They're already overloaded.'

The second part of that statement may well be true, but the first is not. Employee surveys routinely rank 'feeling included' as one of the key factors in job satisfaction (well above salary, for instance). You can't feel included if you don't know what's going on.

We live in a world where information is all around us. We're used to being able to find it and act on it any time we want: buying groceries, booking concert tickets, checking obscure quiz facts. This makes our lives easier. Why would it make sense for us to have easy access to information everywhere except at work?

It's not true that your employees want less information. What they want is *better* information – information that's relevant and useful to them – and the ability to access it when they choose, not have it imposed on them.

Let's just pause for a moment and think about how most of your employees get their information when they're not in work. In fact, let's divide it into four basic information needs: news, facts, conversation and transaction.

When your employees read information on a news website, it's been crafted by experts to make it tight and relevant. If they're not interested, they don't read it.

When they check the value of their investments or the weather forecast, they're much less interested in style and context; they just want the facts, quickly and easily. If the process is slow or difficult, they'll get frustrated and go somewhere else.

When they read a friend's post on facebook, they don't mind if it's rambling or badly-written, because they're interested in the content and they like the sender enough to make allowances for their style. But, if they're not interested or don't like the sender, they won't bother to read it.

When they buy something online, they expect the experience to be easy and intuitive. If it isn't, they probably won't use that site again.

So far, so obvious, you might think.

The problem comes when they go to work.

Let's take the same user-needs we identified just now – news, facts, conversation, transactions – and translate them into a workplace environment.

When was the last time you saw any corporate news source – a physical or digital publication, intranet or email bulletin – where you were interested in most (or even any) of the stories?

How easy do you think most businesses make it for people to find the facts they want, without having to wade through loads of stuff that isn't relevant?

How many corporate attempts to set up social media networks really catch hold – and how many fizzle out after a few months, because people don't really see the point?

When was the last time you heard anyone praising the intuitive user-friendliness of their organisation's online expenses management or holiday booking applications?

And how often, when there's an important issue that employees really want to know about (potential job losses, for instance), is there absolute corporate radio silence?

The reason why so much internal communication feels like noise is not because people don't want information. It's because the information isn't presented to them in a way that means anything.

Forget about the medium – focus on the message

In many ways, internal communicators have never had it so good. The range and sophistication of channels available to them – particularly digital channels – is growing all the time.

But, in the rush to keep up with the latest technology, is there a risk of something more important being overlooked?

Over the last ten years, I've watched a lot of companies replace their printed employee newsletter with a digital channel, because surveys told them that employees found the newsletter 'boring' and 'irrelevant'.

Unfortunately, the content they now put on the digital channel is the same as the content they used to put in their newsletter. It's still boring and irrelevant. All they've done is make it easier for people to ignore.

Philip Davies, of brand consultants Siegel & Gale, says the simplest forms of communication are usually the best:

'Brands that only use the channels they need – and don't try to use all the new, shiny toys just because they can – tend to be the most effective. Berkshire Hathaway is totally stripped down in the way it communicates, but it has a very clear sense of who it's talking to and what they want to know. That's why it's one of the strongest brands out there.'

My own agency recently carried out a research study to

understand what employees think of the internal communication in their organisation. We spoke to around two thousand employees in a variety of different job roles and business types. This is what we found:

First, the most popular channels tend to be the simplest: nothing beats face-to-face conversations with well-informed managers or supervisors.

Second, the choice of channel is always secondary to the quality of content. People are used to being able to access information when and how they want it in their personal lives, so it makes sense that they would want the same flexibility and choice in their working lives. But they expect it to be good.

You might like reading newspapers, but that doesn't mean you'd read the free local paper that gets shoved through your letterbox once a week. The same applies to a printed employee newsletter: whatever your normal reading habits, you'll only read it if you believe it'll be interesting. If it looks and feels like a parish newsletter, people will assume it's amateur and treat the information in it accordingly.

Similarly, you might like getting all your information through your smartphone, with email alerts prompting you to click through to news stories. But you won't click on a work-related news link if you don't think it'll be worth reading. That's why what you say is more important than where you say it.

The third theme emerging from the research is that people expect to be treated as grown-ups. They like having access to senior managers. They like to feel involved. And, above all, they hate feeling like information is not being shared with them.

This is an important point, because there's often a default assumption in organisations that the way to cut down noise is to communicate less: 'we don't want to drown our people in comms, so let's switch some of it off.'

That's a bit like one partner in a relationship deciding 'nothing I say seems to be right, so the best thing I can do is say nothing.'

If you stop communicating, the relationship dies. What you really need to do is not communicate less, but communicate better: be more succinct, more relevant, more interesting, more open. And, above all, think about the other person's perspective before you open your mouth.

Focus on the out*come*. Not the out*put*.

The single biggest reason why the internal communication doesn't work in most companies is because the people doing it are concentrating on the out*put (what we tell our people)* rather than the outcome *(what those people think and feel)*.

This is because the output is tangible. You can count words, you can see intranet pages, you can look at conference slides. You know your comms team is being busy.

Yet the truth is that most of the output is not very good. There's generally way too much of it. It tends to be transactional and dull. When it tries to be more engaging, it often misses the mark and ends up sounding phoney.

Look around you at the communication in your own organisation: the intranet, the publications, the CEO blog, the departmental briefings, the video updates, the management conference.

Be honest: how much of it would you read or listen to if you didn't have to?

How much of it compares favourably with the media you choose in your life away from work? And how much of it is just creating more noise?

You can't communicate with people who aren't listening.

If you want your audience to listen, you have to make it worth their while.

In a nutshell...

#6 Turn down the background noise

'Noise' is bad for productivity: people who are interrupted take 50% longer to complete a task – and make 50% more mistakes. Organisations that encourage positive ways to help employees focus have seen significant performance improvements as a result.

DO...

...insist that people prepare properly before they communicate: simplifying their points and making them relevant to the audience, rather than just drowning them with data.

DON'T...

...stop communicating. Your employees don't want less information – they want better information.

Secret #7:
Make it simple

Ben Hunt-Davis is an Olympic rower. In May 1998, he and his fellow oarsmen in the GB Eight had just finished a disappointing seventh in the Cologne regatta.

Admittedly, they hadn't been far off the pace – and they had been up against the best teams in the world – but this felt like a particularly low moment. They were all talented rowers, they'd all worked incredibly hard and made big sacrifices over a period of years, they had a good coach and good equipment. But somehow, they just couldn't seem to translate it into medal-winning performances.

They knew something had to change: if they carried on doing what they were doing, they'd just keep on getting the sixth and seventh place finishes they'd been getting.

So they sat down as a team to talk about it, which is when one of the eight made a deceptively simple observation: 'We just need to make the boat go faster.'

It was like flicking a switch. From that moment, every decision anyone in the crew made – from what they ate, to the kit they used, to training techniques – was judged in relation to that one question: 'Will it make the boat go faster?' If the answer was no, they didn't do it. Simple.

Over the next two years, this ruthless focus on carving out incremental gains gradually helped them close the gap on their rivals. From sixth and seventh place finishes, they began challenging for medals.

Finally, in September 2000, came the race of their lives. With the whole world watching, Ben Hunt-Davis and the GB Eight beat the best rowers in the world – the same crews who'd beaten them two years earlier – to win Gold at the Sydney Olympics.

They'd made the boat go faster.

What's your OBT (One Big Thing)?

These days, Ben Hunt-Davis is a motivational speaker and business consultant, based in London. His business helps companies all over the world to apply the same lessons that worked so well for the GB Eight. And he's written a best-selling book, called (of course) *Will it make the boat go faster?*

'It's about simplicity and focus,' says Hunt-Davis. 'We all tend to get caught up doing the things in front of us. So we waste a lot of time doing things that don't make a difference, when what we need to do is focus on the one or two things that really matter.'

Of course, the hardest part is often working out what those one or two things are in the first place.

One of the organisations that got it right was Southwest Airlines: the original template for all the budget carriers, such as Easyjet, RyanAir and Air Asia, that have revolutionised short-haul air travel in the last 25 years.

Herb Kelleher, who set up the airline in 1971 and turned it into one of the most admired and successful companies in the world, gave his employees one very simple mantra for making decisions: 'Will it make us the low cost airline? If it won't, we don't do it.'

The trick is to take something complex and explain it in terms that will help your employees make better decisions. This is one of the most important jobs your internal communication should be doing for you – and the rationale for doing it well couldn't be clearer.

Siegel & Gale is a consultancy that specialises in helping businesses to simplify their brand and customer experience. Every year, they publish a global simplicity index, highlighting the brands that are best at making it easy for customers to understand, choose and buy their products and services.

Their research shows that, in an increasingly-complex world, 64% of consumers are willing to pay more for a simpler experience. 61% are more likely to recommend a brand because it's simple. Those are commercially very significant numbers.

Siegel & Gale's UK head Philip Davies says the consumer's perception of simplicity is now far more to do with experience than with marketing:

'The days of advertising as the only way of explaining yourself are over. The way to explain yourself now is by experience. That's about people – and people don't always behave logically and rationally. So you need to temper the rational approach with a bit of instinct and emotion.'

Simplicity is good for the share price, too: a portfolio of the top 10 brands in Siegel & Gale's index would outperform the FTSE index by around 400%.

By contrast, more complex businesses find themselves having to invest more time and resources into handling and resolving customer queries.

So it seems pretty obvious that any sane organisation would want to find ways of simplifying the way it works for both customers and employees.

And yet most employees in most businesses have precisely the opposite experience. How come?

Strategy is sacrifice

When you're making a TV commercial, the air-time is expensive and you only have a few seconds to make your point – so you have to be absolutely single-minded about what you're going to say.

The airtime on the inside of your business is much cheaper, so most organisations aren't nearly as disciplined with their internal messages. There's a tendency to say as much as possible, on the assumption that, the more points you can make in favour of a project, the easier it will be to persuade people to support you.

That's a big mistake, because it actually has the opposite effect. It makes your messages less clear and it makes your priorities confused: the more things you give people to think about, the harder it is for them to know what matters.

(It's also a financial mistake because, if you were to tot up all the working time wasted by ineffective communication, you'd quickly realise it's costing you a lot more than you think it is).

That's why I believe the single biggest lesson internal communication can learn from advertising is focus. Advertising legend David Ogilvy had a phrase that sums this up very neatly: 'Strategy is sacrifice'.

The idea is that, to be effective, communication needs to focus on a single, clear message. That's much harder than it sounds, because there's a natural, human temptation to want to tell all the good stuff. 'It's all important', you think. 'How can I leave any of it out?'

And yet, the more you tell people, the more you give them to think about, the less clear your message will be – and the less likely they are to think or do what you want them to.

They're also a lot less likely to be engaged with your brand or your ambitions, whereas Siegel & Gale's research shows that 62% of employees in companies perceived to be simple can be considered 'brand champions'. Simplicity works – and it delivers better results.

The New Zealand rugby team, the All Blacks, is the most consistently successful team in sporting history. One of the key reasons for their success is their determination not to overcomplicate things.

When giving feedback to players, the management team is careful to focus on a maximum of two areas for improvement. This makes it easier for players to be clear about what they need to do.

They also focus relentlessly on basic skills, such as catching and passing – carrying out many of the same drills you see being practised by under-11 teams all over the country.

It may feel unsophisticated, but the endless hours of drilling make the skills second nature: in the pivotal moments of big games, when the pressure is on, the All Blacks can always be relied on to execute these basic skills accurately. They make far fewer mistakes under pressure – and that is often what makes the difference between winning and losing.

If you can't draw it, it's too complicated

Take a look at this sketch.

It's not very pretty and it's not by a famous artist. But you could make a strong case for describing it as the most valuable picture ever created.

It was drawn by the British Admiral Horatio Nelson in 1805, on the eve of the battle of Trafalgar. He had invited his captains on board HMS Victory for dinner. As the main course was being cleared away, he gathered them round the table to outline his battle plan, which he sketched out with the few quick strokes of his pen that you see here.

Nelson used the sketch to illustrate a simple, but critical, point. Instead of sailing in a line parallel with the Franco-Spanish fleet and simply pounding away in an exchange of gunfire (the orthodox naval tactics of the time), he wanted his ships to sail straight at the enemy, break their line and engage them at close quarters.

It was risky, but it was also the only way to achieve a decisive victory. Sticking to the rule-book would be unlikely to give either fleet much of an advantage. Whereas getting in close would allow the superior seamanship and gunnery of the British crews to come into their own.

The stakes were high: if Nelson failed and his fleet was beaten, the one obstacle preventing a French invasion of Britain would be removed. On the other hand, a decisive victory would give the British naval supremacy (in those days, as significant an advantage as air supremacy is in today's conflicts).

Success depended on his captains understanding what they had to do and executing it perfectly. Luckily, Nelson was an instinctive communicator. He knew that, if he just explained his plan in a speech, his officers would hear him, but might assume they'd misunderstood, because what he was saying was unusual. So, by drawing a few lines on a sheet of paper, he removed any possibility of misunderstanding.

His captains got it immediately. The plan worked: the French and Spanish were comprehensively routed and Britain established a dominance of the seas that would last for the next hundred years.

What was that worth?

Well, at the height of its Empire, in 1860, Britain accounted for a staggering 47% of all global trade. (To put that figure in context, today's most active trading nation, China, accounts for around 17%).

That trading dominance was only possible because of the Royal Navy's absolute control of the seas. Which, in turn, was only possible because of the decisive victory at Trafalgar.

Which makes Nelson's sketch worth around $100 trillion in today's money.

Eat your heart out, Damien Hirst.

Pictures trump words

According to John Medina, the molecular biologist and author of *Brain Rules,* the likelihood of us hearing a piece of information and remembering it three days later is about 10% on average. If you add a picture, that likelihood goes up to 65%.

In other words, we're *six and a half times* more likely to remember the picture than the words. (Which is a useful fact to keep in mind when you're planning your next presentation).

There's a fairly simple explanation for why this should be the case. Our brains process words and pictures in exactly the same way. As pictures.

To our brain, every word is a collection of individual pictures – or letters, as we call them – and it has to work just as hard processing one letter as it does processing one picture. If you put up a slide with forty words on it, you're making your audience work too hard.

This is not something that will come as a surprise to the Millennial generation. Young people entering the workforce now have grown up in a world of visual communication, where everyone has cameras on their smartphones and a choice of social media platforms to share their pictures instantly.

More than 10% of all the photographs ever taken were taken in the last twelve months. That's not because technology has changed our instincts. Quite the opposite: it's made it easy and cheap for us to communicate in the way that's always been most natural.

The real power of pictures, however, comes when we combine them with our other senses. The more senses we use to communicate information, the greater the chance that the audience will take it on board and remember it.

Film, for instance, is particularly powerful, because it allows you to combine pictures, not just with words, but with music as well. If you get it right, that's a big emotional hit (although the wrong music or mismatched pictures can make it fall flat on its face).

Make the data make sense

The last ten years have seen a massive increase in the popularity of the infographic and that trend is only likely to continue.

When it's done well, it's an immensely powerful thing: the wonderful *Information is Beautiful* is packed with examples (if you haven't read it, by the way, I urge you to get a copy – or just have a look at the website: informationisbeautiful.net).

Apart from anything else, the process of turning complex numerical data into a single image forces you to be simple. It makes you think about the information in the way your audience might think about it. It forces you to delve into the mountain of data and pull out the one key point or pattern that explains exactly why it matters. And it allows you to express it in a way that your audience is likely to grasp.

The best ideas can always be articulated simply. As Einstein memorably put it: 'If you can't explain it to a child of six, you don't understand it yourself.'

That's why you should be wary of any presentation that deals in bullet points: high word-count is a sure sign that the presenter hasn't thought about their subject clearly enough to identify the real point. Whereas, if they can draw a picture to explain it, they probably have.

Michael Loeve is a Danish retailer. In 2012, he was made CEO of the ailing SuperBrugsen supermarket chain – part of the Danish Co-operative Group – with a brief to revive its fortunes in the face of growing pressure from discounters.

Loeve quickly realised that SuperBrugsen had two big problems. The first was price, but that was resolved fairly easily. The second – and trickier – problem was the way SuperBrugsen's stores felt to customers. They were cluttered and confusing – with a bewildering array of products and a mass of different signage, displays and promotional offers. Interestingly, no-one inside SuperBrugsen had identified this as a problem.

Along with the heads of the Co-op's other retail businesses,

Loeve was invited to make a brief presentation to the Group Board, outlining his plan for turning his business around.

Each CEO had just five minutes to present. While the other business heads tried to squeeze as many bullet points as possible into a couple of slides, Loeve took a simpler approach.

He started with a picture he'd taken inside a supermarket in Spain. It was very clean and uncluttered, with clear lines of sight and simple signposting making it easy and appealing to shop. The Board nodded approvingly.

Then, one by one, Loeve layered onto the picture all the elements that you'd find in a typical SuperBrugsen store: displays, signage, pallets of promotional stock. Each of these elements had a perfectly justifiable reason for being there – but, lumped together, they looked messy, confusing and unappealing. A lot less shopper-friendly than the picture he'd started with. The Board frowned.

Then, gradually, one by one, he unpicked the elements until he got back to the view of the store that he wanted to create: much simpler and cleaner.

The Board got it immediately: it had taken Michael Loeve a little over two minutes to articulate a problem that the business had been wrestling with for years – and to get the green light for his solution.

Over the next few weeks, he used the same picture to explain to the rest of the business what they needed to achieve and why.

Within a few months, SuperBrugsen was getting much higher customer ratings for its shopping experience. Within a year, it was recording double-digit growth.

Because everybody had a really clear picture of what they needed to do.

Pictures and emotions

Unsurprisingly, Michael Loeve remains a big fan of using images to explain ideas.

Where other CEOs might have a hotline to the ad agency for those occasions when they need help articulating what needs to change, Loeve prefers to call his favourite cartoonist.

'Cartoons are a good way to pose difficult questions, because they allow you to exaggerate feelings in a way that feels lighter than a photograph or a bullet point. You're not attacking anyone. You're just saying *'hey, look at this thing we're doing – how do we feel about this?'* That lightness makes it easier for people to accept.'

It's an approach that has become surprisingly familiar to medical students in Chicago, many of whom are now learning how to draw comics as part of their studies.

The idea is to help future doctors relate more naturally to their patients by making them think about the words they use and the impact those words have on patients.

It's the brain-child of MK Czerwiec, a graphic artist and former HIV nurse, who found that drawing comics helped her articulate her own emotional response to difficult cases – as well as understanding how the patients and their families would have been feeling. If you're interested, you can find examples at graphicmedicine.org.

Comic strips have long been regarded as a much more serious form of communication in countries like France and Japan than they have in the UK and US. But we're catching up: graphic novels are growing in popularity – and the film industry is latching on to them. (Which is not surprising: the story-telling structure of comics and films is very similar. In fact, when making his film of the adventures of Tintin, Director Stephen Spielberg commented that it was easy to shoot because the storyboard was already there).

Presentations work – or, at least, should work – in a very similar way.

When I'm helping clients prepare for presentations, the advice I always give them is to imagine they're a news presenter. Their job is to tell the story and the job of what appears on screen is to illustrate that story: a picture, a graphic, maybe a piece of film – and, only very rarely, a few words that you might want to punch out for extra emphasis.

Presenters don't always like hearing this. Many of them feel much more comfortable when they've got bullet-points and lots of different things on the screen at the same time. More content makes their life easier, they tell me: it helps them remember all the things they wanted to say.

They're missing the point. Presentations, like films or comics, are not about detail. They're about belief and an emotional connection.

Having more detail on the screen may make it easier for the presenter, but it makes it a lot harder for the audience. Their brains are having to do much more processing than if they were just looking at a picture and listening to a clear, compelling story.

If you can't do that for them, then you haven't got the story straight in your own head. And no amount of technical pizzazz is going to fix that problem for you.

In a nutshell...

#7 Make it simple

Giving people more information does not make it easier for them to make good decisions. Businesses that score highly for simplicity outperform more complex businesses by a significant margin.

DO...

...be very clear about the one big thing you want to achieve (like the Olympic rowing team whose mantra was 'will it make the boat go faster?')

DON'T...

...allow people to get away with bullet-points. If they can't illustrate the point they want to make with an image or drawing, it's too complicated.

Secret #8:
Be interesting

At the Edinburgh Festival Fringe, there's a competition called 'So you think you're funny', where up-and-coming comics tout their wares in front of a live audience. Many of the UK's leading comedians have used it as a platform to launch their careers, but it's not for the faint-hearted.

According to Irish comic Jason Byrne – one of those who survived and thrived in the cauldron of the competition – success is all about your connection with the audience.

'Basically, you've got three seconds to win the audience over. If you do that, you can say almost anything and they'll laugh, because they like you. If you don't, there's really no way back.'

Interestingly, Byrne also says that the decision to like you or not is very rarely based on a rational assessment of how funny you are.

'You get comedians who sit there afterwards and complain. They say 'my material's way better than his' – but it doesn't matter. The audience isn't responding on a rational level – it's instinctive and emotional.'

Sophie Scott is another stand-up comedian. She's also a

professor of cognitive neuroscience at London's prestigious UCL University, who has carved out a significant global profile for her pioneering work in the study of laghter.

She says the most important thing to understand about laughter is that it's really a sign of appreciation:

'If you go to a comedy show in Tokyo, London and New York, you'll see the audience express its amusement in very different ways: the Brits will laugh and look around them to check everyone else is laughing too; the Americans will whoop and holler; the Japanese will clap politely.'

In other words, the laughter is not an unconscious reaction. It's a collective stamp of approval: an acknowledgement that the performer is saying, or doing, something that we like the idea of.

So what fits into that category: what do we find funny?

'Humour can be about anything,' says Professor Scott. 'But it's nearly always based in truth. We admire cleverness: people who are quirky and inventive with language. And clarity: people who can simplify complex things in order to point out how absurd they are. And free thinking: people who challenge taboos, who question society, who find ways of articulating what we all secretly think.'

Let's pause for a moment and apply that to a work context. How much of the communication in your office would you say falls into the categories outlined above? How much feels true? How much feels clever? How much feels like it's simplifying complex things – or articulating what everyone thinks?

And what can we learn from stand-up comedians about how to make our communication more engaging?

1. Look the part

When Sophie Scott started doing stand-up, the first lesson she learned was about 'microphone etiquette': always leaving the microphone centre stage and at the right height, ready for the next act.

'People get very cross with you if you don't,' she says. 'It's because audiences make very quick, subconscious judgements about performers. If you come on stage and spend the first few seconds fiddling about, trying to adjust the height of the microphone – or get it out of its stand – they think you don't know what you're doing. It's hard to recover from that.'

The same rules apply in a business context: you need to reassure the audience that you belong there. If you don't follow your own brand guidelines, if your presentation is amateurish, or if your eyes keep wandering when you're speaking to camera, you'll kill your credibility. And, if you do that, it doesn't matter how good your material is: people won't be listening.

2. Don't make your audience work too hard

The best comics make it sound like their material is a thought that just occurred to them. But, in most cases, they've been working on it for months: trying it out, refining it, changing a word here and a word there and polishing it, until they're confident it's as powerful as possible.

The result is that it all feels very easy for the audience: you feel like you're having a conversation with a smarter, more insightful, more articulate version of yourself.

A lot of this is to do with empathy and rapport: the choice of examples, the use of language – all of this helps to establish a connection with the audience and a sense of relevance to their lives.

A good comedian makes you think 'Yes, I recognise what you're talking about' – even when they're talking about something you've never thought about before.

It's the same when you're communicating in a business: you need to make it easy for people to relate to what you're telling them, even if it's something they've never thought about before.

3. Have a good punchline

We've already talked about the three seconds you've got to win the audience over. The impression you leave them with is every bit as important.

Most comedians build their act so that it closes with some kind of climactic pay-off: you want to save your best joke till last, so you can shout 'thank you, you've been a wonderful audience' over a cacophony of applause.

That doesn't mean you need to sign off every intranet article with a climactic gag. But it does mean that, wherever possible, you should aim to finish with a pithy reminder of the point you want your audience to take away.

This is particularly true of presentations, which so often start with a bang and then fizzle out into an aimless mass of detail.

Much better to follow the structure that works for comedians: start with something attention-grabbing; build your points in a tight and logical sequence (not one word more than necessary); then finish with a flourish on the one big thing you want your audience to remember.

Putting together a presentation like that takes a lot more effort (there's no slide template for a 'brief, insightful summary'), but the audience will thank you for it.

4. Involve the audience

Good stand-up comedy is seldom one-way. Comedians feed off the audience: sometimes overtly ('any Australians in the crowd tonight...?') and sometimes more subtly ('have you ever wondered...?')

This is because they know their best chance of engaging the audience is to make them a part of the show.

Organisations that actively involve their employees in developing their culture tend to have more engaged employees – think John Lewis or Nordstrom or Google.

But you can't build that kind of culture overnight and you can't fake it with a quick feedback session. You need to earn your audience's trust over time.

5. Be emotional

The brain pays much more attention to information with an emotional impact: it prompts a surge of dopamine, which makes that information easier for your brain to retrieve. This is why you can remember events from your childhood with astonishing clarity, but you can't remember where you left your car keys last night.

Stand-up comics tell stories that help their audience connect with their feelings (often feelings of awkwardness or embarrassment – how often do you see the camera at a live show cut to someone hiding their eyes as they laugh?)

If you want your audience to engage with your communication, don't just fill it with facts and numbers. People don't relate to numbers: they relate to feelings.

6. Be specific

Very few stand-ups can get away with talking about abstract ideas. It's much more common to introduce the idea ('have you ever noticed how...?') and then immediately switch to a specific example ('the other day, I was making a cup of tea and my Mum said...')

In the same way, companies like Nordstrom use individual stories to provide a meaningful example of the behaviour they want to encourage.

It's a lot more engaging than a check-list of abstract value statements ('integrity', 'openness', 'customer focus'...). And, because it's about people like them, it's a lot more likely to prompt others to want to emulate it.

7. Be unexpected

We tend to think we're in charge of our brains, but it's really the other way round – and that's just as well. If we consciously processed all the information involved in even the simplest task (like catching a ball or putting a fork into our mouths), we'd be overwhelmed. We depend on our sub-conscious brains to sift through all that information and dump whatever we don't need to know.

The brain's reaction is to focus on looking for new, or unexpected, information. It filters out what it already knows, on the basis that it's not likely to represent either a threat or an opportunity that we need to be aware of.

In other words, what's easy for writing (set templates, cut and paste content) is hopeless for making your message memorable. Things that look and sound familiar are more likely to be ignored by your audience's sub-conscious brain.

That's why good stand-ups always look for a different angle, for a way to subvert the familiar and force the brain to pay attention.

You should do the same when you're communicating in your business – but be careful. The classic internal comms mistake is to make something 'whacky' or 'fun' or 'shocking' in a bid to get the audience's attention. This won't work unless it also feels relevant.

8. What's in it for me?

Perhaps the single most important lesson is that, if you want people to pay attention, you have to make it worth their while.

In comedy, the payoff is in the humour: you pay attention and you get the joke. But, in corporate communication, you're not likely to be looking for laughs, so you need to find other ways of making your point relevant.

One of my favourite examples of this is the fly you'll find painted on every urinal in the men's bathrooms in Amsterdam's Schiphol Airport.

The flies are there because airport bosses had become concerned about the amount of time and money being spent on cleaning round the urinals. It turned out male passengers were too distracted or in too much of a hurry to pay attention to their aim. Over time, these little spillages added up to a sizeable cleaning bill and a fairly unpleasant experience for travellers.

The airport's facilities team had tried a number of different ways to encourage urinal-users to be more fastidious: from polite cajoling to threatening notices to spot fines. Nothing seemed to make any difference.

Then someone came up with the idea of painting a fly on the

urinals. Men are instinctively competitive creatures, they reasoned. If you give them rational reasons to improve their aim, they'll just tune them out. Whereas, if you give them a target to aim at, they won't want to miss.

The difference was immediate and spectacular. Cleaning costs in the trial urinal areas fell dramatically. And, since the flies have been rolled out to the rest of the airport, the savings now run into millions of Euros.

If you want people to pay attention, give them a reason they care about.

In a nutshell...

#8 Be interesting

You can't bore people into paying attention: you have to make it worth their while. Learn from stand-up comedians: look the part, have a good punchline and get your audience involved.

DO...

...bring your points to life. Use examples your audience can easily understand and relate to: human stories, not dry facts and abstract ideas.

DON'T...

...make the audience work too hard: if you want them to get your point, you need to do the heavy lifting for them.

Secret #9:
Be Real

I've lost count of the number of corporate presentations I've been to where senior executives claim to be 'passionate' about something (including paperclips, wall cladding and dog deodorisers). 'Passion' is a word that has been used so often and so inappropriately, for so long, that most people have learned to tune it out.

If you're really passionate about something, your passion is obvious: you don't need to talk about it, because people can feel it – and because you let it guide your actions even when doing so may harm your interests.

As Bill Bernbach, the godfather of modern advertising, once put it: 'A principle isn't a principle until it costs you money.'

Anita Roddick, who founded the Body Shop, was once advised by her legal department to stop using the word 'activist', because people might associate it with terrorism. Her response was to use the word as often and as publicly as she could – she even launched a perfume called *Activist*. As far as Roddick was concerned, active participation in causes and debate was an essential part of what made Body Shop what it was: she'd rather risk offending people and jeopardising sales than compromise her principles.

During the 1991 Gulf War, Roddick sponsored an anti-war campaign (which, at the time, was a fairly unpopular position for anyone to adopt, let alone the CEO of a public corporation). She faced strong pressure from investors and her own marketing team, who were worried that her stance would damage public support for the brand.

Roddick opened the issue up to all Body Shop employees in a public debate. Had she lost, she would have stepped down. Fortunately for the business, she didn't have to: employees responded to her because the principles Body Shop stood for mattered as much to them as they did to her.

How many CEOs would have the guts to do something that would cost them money and might cost them their job, just because it was the right thing to do?

No-one in Body Shop had the slightest doubt, while Anita Roddick was around, what the business believed in.

That's passion.

Why it's important to remember your mistakes

Barely a week goes by without some corporate behaviour horror story splattered across the news: banks fined for rigging exchange rates, pharmaceutical companies fined for trying to bribe doctors, executives at world football's governing body arrested for bribing each other.

In the Autumn of 2015, news broke that German car giant Volkswagen had been caught cheating the emissions tests for its diesel cars in the United States. Investigators discovered that the car exhausts were fitted with smart software that could detect when a test was being carried out and adjust the car's performance electronically to give better results.

It was front page news all over the world. Volkswagen's management seemed genuinely horrified by what had happened. The company's US chief made a grovelling apology to the investigating senate committee. The CEO stepped down and his successor immediately took out contrite full page advertisements in newspapers in every major market, apologising unreservedly to customers and vowing to win back their trust.

A swift internal investigation concluded that the test-rigging software had been created by a few 'rogue' engineers – and the company announced it was taking robust steps to make sure this could never happen again.

The problem was that it already had.

In 1973, Volkswagen faced a similar accusation from US

investigators that it had been rigging tests and, although the company admitted no wrongdoing, it made a $120,000 payment in settlement (quite a lot of money at the time).

Whether you believe VW's story about the rogue engineers or not, the point is that no lessons were learned from the mistakes of the past. The corporate memory had been expunged, leaving nothing to prevent VW making the same mistakes all over again (although, this time, with rather more serious consequences).

It's an example of the *realpolitik* involved in being a public corporation. Business leaders are under constant pressure to deliver growth, even when the market is flat and competition is fierce. In order to stand out, they feel compelled to make promises that are increasingly hard to deliver – knowing that, if they don't deliver, they'll be fired. So their focus becomes all about delivering the promise: pressure is pushed downward through the organisation and ethics are quietly marginalised in the quest to make the impossible possible. In that kind of short-term hot-house environment, there's no room for uncomfortable lessons from the past.

Companies have been taught by their PR agencies to own up to their mistakes – just as VW's management has had to do. But only when they're past the point of plausible denial. And, once the crisis has passed, their tendency is to sweep everything under the carpet and 'move on': start again with a clean slate (and probably a new leadership team) and never mention the problem again. Negative stories are frowned on. Inconvenient truths are forgotten.

Which is a pity. Because the only way to avoid making the same mistakes in the future is to make sure people remember them.

Trust starts with truth

Black Box Thinking is a book by British journalist Matthew Syed, whose central theme is that a willingness to embrace failure is the only way organisations can improve their performance. The title comes from the black box flight recorder used to establish the cause of aeroplane disasters.

Syed's point is that encouraging people to speak openly – and without fear of retribution – about the things that go wrong is the best way to learn from them.

After the Columbia space shuttle disaster in 2003, NASA were so determined to make sure it would never happen again that they made the case study a part of the induction for every new recruit. It's a level of honesty and self-awareness that a lot of businesses could benefit from.

Syed cites a Harvard Business Review report, where the executives interviewed believed that less than 5% of the failures in their business were actually blameworthy. When asked how many mistakes were treated as blameworthy, the answer was over 70%.

This tendency to apportion blame – to 'make people accountable' for things they can't actually control – is why most organisations find it impossible to establish a culture of trust. It's why people are terrified to speak openly about things that don't work – which is why, in turn, it's so hard to learn the lessons that would prevent those things going wrong in future.

It's a kind of organisational *omerta*, and it's often seen at its most extreme in the field of healthcare, where fear of litigation has created a culture of cover-up and silence. Gradually, however, the pendulum is beginning to swing the other way – and there's one shining example of what can happen when you embrace failure.

Virginia Mason hospital in Seattle has a scheme called Patient Safety Alerts, which encourage staff members to report problems and mistakes whenever they happen. The idea is to identify the gaps in process or skills that are allowing mistakes to be made, so that they can be corrected.

The key element in the scheme is that there are no repercussions for the people who make the reports: the policy is motivated entirely by a desire to improve rather than to blame.

The result is a much greater degree of openness, where people willingly highlight their own mistakes – unheard of in a US medical environment where individuals, as well as institutions, are frequently the target of personal injury lawsuits.

Cathie Furman is the hospital's senior vice-president of quality and compliance. In an interview for the Daily Telegraph, she explained that Patient Safety Alerts have helped to make Virginia Mason a much safer place.

'In healthcare around the world, the culture has been one of blame and hierarchy. That makes it very difficult to find out what needs to be fixed: you can't understand something you hide. We're safer because we're finding out.'

Every month, Furman's team handles between 800 and 1,000 alerts, highlighting everything from a missed diagnosis to a missing soap dispenser: anything that might possibly affect patient safety is highlighted and questioned.

Initially, there was resistance to the change. When the Safety Alerts were first introduced in 2002, very few staff came forward: even with the promise of no repercussions, they didn't want to get colleagues in trouble or open themselves up to potential litigation.

The catalyst for change was a tragic mistake in November 2004, when a 69-year old mother of four was accidentally injected with a toxic antiseptic instead of a harmless marker dye during a brain operation. The liquids were both clear and both contained in identical, unmarked steel cups: the syringe was filled from the wrong cup.

It was an accident that could have happened anywhere, but the consequences were terrible: the patient's condition deteriorated rapidly and, 19 days later, she died.

Instead of pursuing a course of denial and damage limitation, the hospital's management immediately accepted full responsibility – and the staff were sufficiently shocked that they wanted to make sure nothing like it would ever happen again. In the aftermath of the death, Patient Safety Alerts began pouring in.

What about the lawsuits? In a nation as litigious as the United States, you might expect a policy of admitting mistakes to lead to an increase in negligence claims.

In fact, the opposite has happened: Virginia Mason has seen its liability insurance premiums come down by 74%. It turns out that what most people want is an apology and the reassurance that the hospital cares enough to make sure it never happens again.

You need to stop the machine getting in the way

Unfortunately, the story isn't always quite so positive.

A friend of mine is a midwife. Recently, she had to deal with an emergency: a man ran in to the maternity ward where she was working, panicking because his wife was giving birth in the car outside. Sue hurried out to the car with him and, realising that it was a breach birth and it wasn't safe to move the mother, finished delivering the baby in the car, removed the umbilical cord that was choking it, wrapped it in a blanket and rushed it upstairs to the waiting doctors.

Thanks to her swift intervention, the baby survived and is now a healthy, happy child with an eternally grateful mother. For Sue, however, it was the start of a long and demoralising disciplinary process, as she was made to explain why she had acted in a way that was not in line with correct procedure.

Correct procedure was not to get involved. Correct procedure was to call an ambulance, then wait while it turned up and the paramedics could assess the situation and decide what action to take. That was the peer-approved, risk-assessed, legally compliant way to respond to the emergency. If my friend had followed correct procedure, there would have been no risk that the hospital or health service could be sued in the event of something going wrong.

But the baby would have died.

How could that possibly be the right outcome?

Lord Price – the UK Trade Minister and former Deputy Chairman of the John Lewis Partnership – describes this phenomenon as 'the machine'.

'The machine makes people do things they don't want to do. Every time you find yourself doing or saying something that you know isn't right, it's the machine – and, the more you let the machine influence the decisions in your business, the less likely you are to succeed.'

Price says a lot of the John Lewis Partnership's success is down to the fact that the people who work in it also own it – so the decisions they make are based on what their friends and colleagues would think, rather than what outside shareholders might want. They have an instinctive understanding of what the right thing is to do in any situation.

It's a characteristic you often come across when you talk to people in high-performing teams, from business to sport to the military. When they're making decisions, their most important point of reference is their colleagues: they respect them, they trust them and they don't want to disappoint them.

Which is why team-building – by which I mean real team-building, not an occasional awkward day on an assault course –

is such a vital component of any working environment.

Whole Foods Market is a large chain of organic food shops. It started in 1980, with one shop and 19 employees, and now employs more than 80,000 people in 380 stores across the US, Canada and UK.

CEO and founder John Mackey is a big believer in the value of team culture. He encourages senior managers to spend time with employees outside the business and regularly does the same himself: staying over at colleagues' houses and getting to know their families. The result is that the work relationship feels much more real: you get to know people as people, rather than a work function.

New employees spend two months with a team as a probationary period. At the end of that two months, the other members of the team hold a secret ballot: they have to be approved by at least two-thirds of the team or they won't be kept on.

It's a strongly consensual culture, with many decisions devolved to store or team level. Mackey admits the result is sometimes less efficient, with ideas being duplicated, but says this is far outweighed by the benefit of an engaged and motivated workforce.

The results bear him out: Whole Foods Market's revenue grew

8% in 2015 and 10% the previous year. Forbes magazine has listed the business as one of the '100 best companies to work for' in each of the past 18 years.

Write like you speak (and speak like a human)

I always hated science at school because of the way we were made to write up experiments. I understood the need for clinical objectivity, but it still seemed very wrong to take something as inherently enjoyable as blowing things up with a Bunsen burner and then strip all the joy out of it: *'the apparatus was connected'; 'heat was applied to the test tube'; 'a combustible reaction was observed'.*

I thought I'd left all that behind when I gave up chemistry at 13. But, if you look around you in almost any company today, you'll find plenty of people who still write as though they're writing their science homework – and then wonder why nobody wants to read it.

You know the kind of thing I'm talking about: formal language, passive tense, an abundance of jargon.

Mind you, it's also possible to go too far the other way.

Over the last twenty years, spin-doctors and focus groups have taught politicians to speak in a more tabloid-friendly way: ordinary words, populist soundbites, folksy, homespun stories.

But, when you scratch beneath the surface, there's not really any substance: words and phrases are carefully chosen to sound meaningful and sincere – but to leave enough room for deniability.

The same thing has begun to happen with brands. Ever since Innocent first hit the supermarket shelves with their quirky and beautifully-written packaging, brands everywhere have been trying to reinvent themselves with a friendlier, more human tone of voice.

The trouble with the Innocent voice is that it's a bit like skinny jeans: not everyone can pull it off. Especially if you're middle-aged and a bit flabby.

We're living through a fascinating shift in the way brands and consumers work. A lot of very big, very established brands are suddenly finding themselves in an awkward place, where the personality and behaviour that built them no longer feels relevant to a growing portion of their potential market.

They're right to see this as a problem – you've only got to look at the accelerating brand failure rates to see why – but trying to sound 'street' is not the solution. The solution is to stop writing science experiments and start writing like you speak when you're being most yourself.

If you want people to connect with your story, you need to make it easy for them.

Start by having a clear picture in your head of who they are (Warren Buffett used to write all Berkshire Hathaway's annual reports as if they were a letter to his sisters).

Talk in words that are natural to both you and them.

Choose simple words over complex words, whoever you're talking to. Winston Churchill (who knew a bit about communication) said 'short words are best – and old words, when short, are best of all.'

Don't use jargon or buzzwords – and don't allow anyone else to use them either.

Don't confuse people by having lots of different messages, tones and styles of communication (we'll talk about this more in the final chapter).

Use short sentences.

Use words and ideas that paint a picture in your audience's head. That doesn't mean you need to use florid, poetic language: the best descriptions usually come from the simplest words. The absolute master of this art was Theodore Seuss Geigel – Dr Seuss. When challenged to write a book that used only the 50 simple words in the approved early learner's vocabulary, he came up with *Green Eggs and Ham*. Over 50 years later, it's still one of the world's most popular children's stories

– and the perfect riposte to anyone who tells you it's not possible to write anything interesting about sheet metal welding or a new stock management system.

Your subject matter may be dull, but there's no reason why you have to be.

In a nutshell...

#9 Be real

If you want people to care about your business, you have to be authentic: this is even more important on the inside than it is on the outside. You can't fake authenticity – or conjure it with a few glib values. Authenticity is about the way you behave and the way you communicate.

DO...

...create an environment where people can tell the truth without fear of repercussions. If you don't, people won't trust you – and you won't be able to engage them.

DON'T...

...hide behind big words. Write like you speak – and speak like a human being.

Secret #10:
Learn to let go

You've probably seen this classic management consultancy puzzle from the 1970s, but you may not remember how to solve it.

What you have to do is connect all the dots, using no more than four straight lines, *without lifting your pen from the paper.*

Have a go (and don't turn the page until you have).

If you've never seen the puzzle before, there's a better than average chance you gave up in frustration. Most of us assume a restriction that wasn't actually imposed: i.e. that the lines have to remain within the box formed by the outer dots. This won't work.

I sometimes use this puzzle in communication workshops. I give the group three minutes to try solving it, then I show them this:

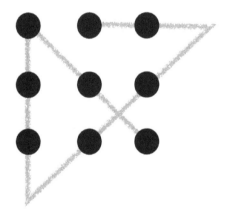

The point is that you can't solve the problem by staying within the obvious frame. You have to go outside the box (which, in case you've ever wondered, is where that particular cliché comes from).

Well done if you figured that out, by the way. Most people don't.

The point of the puzzle is to encourage people to avoid making assumptions and to think about problems more laterally and creatively.

Of course, it's old and fairly well-known now, so you might have seen the solution already. There's usually at least one person in the group who has.

To stop that person feeling smug, my next step is to ask everyone to solve the same puzzle using no more than three lines. Then to do it using just one.

Have a go at those (and don't turn the page till you've finished).

You see, most people (including the management consultants who came up with the puzzle) make a lot more than just one assumption about it.

They also tend to assume that the lines must go straight through the centre of the dots. Whereas, if you're happy just to clip the dots, you can solve the puzzle with three long lines tilted at slight angles.

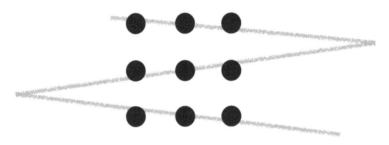

And one line? Well, we never put a restriction on how thick the line could be...

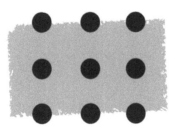

We could go on. After all, nobody said you couldn't fold the paper, or cut the dots out individually and place them side by side...

The point is that, the more restricted your thinking, the less creative your solutions are likely to be.

This is why most businesses are not very creative places. They're hidebound by process, a tendency to default to 'what we feel comfortable with' – and a deep suspicion of time spent thinking rather than doing.

Yet, increasingly, those same businesses are talking about the need to react more quickly – for their people to be confident about making decisions, using their initiative, solving problems.

'We need to be more agile', the planners say. 'We need to empower our people to react to what's going on around them, rather than waiting for instructions.'

The problem is that there's a big difference between knowing what you need and actually making it happen.

Sir Ian Cheshire is the Chairman of Debenhams and one of the most successful British retailers of the last 20 years. He says the most important thing to understand as a leader is that you can't do it yourself.

'You succeed through other people. So your most effective contribution is if you can provide a simple, clear framework and then trust people to get on with it.'

Cheshire calls this 'minimum spec leadership': providing clarity and confidence without paralysing detail.

'If you can give people a few simple rules and then allow them to operate within them, that's your most effective contribution. You're not giving them a bloody great manual of things they've got to do; nor are you abandoning them to complete chaos.'

The trick is to find the right balance.

What we can learn from the Germans

In the closing stages of the second world war, as the Allied armies advanced across Europe, their commanders were astonished by the fighting effectiveness of the German troops they encountered.

Despite being outnumbered and under-resourced, German soldiers consistently outperformed their Allied counterparts. For every 100 German soldiers killed or wounded from D-Day onwards, they managed to kill or wound 142 Allied soldiers in return. In brutal industrial terms, that means the Germans were 42% more productive.

After the war ended, the US army's academics looked into it more closely and discovered that the big difference was in decision-making.

Time and again throughout the war, there were clear instances of the Germans succeeding because small, isolated groups of soldiers under the command of a junior officer or NCO continued to operate effectively, even when they got completely cut off from their command structure. They didn't panic; they didn't sit waiting for orders. They calmly and confidently got on with doing the things their commanders would have wanted them to do. They made good decisions.

This had a lot to do with the concept of *Auftragstaktik,* or 'mission-based tactics', which had been introduced as part of sweeping reforms of the Prussian army in the mid-19th century.

The basic idea of *Auftragstaktik* is that you don't give your subordinates detailed instructions to follow: you tell them what outcome you want to achieve ('by 16.00, I want you to be in control of hill B') and leave it up to them to find the best way to achieve it.

This means your troops can adapt quickly to the confusion of battle and are not constrained by detailed orders that may quickly become unworkable because of unexpected developments on the ground.

Other countries had tried to copy the idea of *Auftragstaktik,* but with much less impressive results. The reason it worked so well in the German army was because the culture and environment were also right.

The man who introduced the reforms, Helmuth von Moltke, had instinctively understood that empowering your subordinates to make their own decisions can only work where there is complete trust both ways.

So his most important contribution was to introduce a genuine element of democracy and fairness into the Prussian army. Where officers had previously been drawn from aristocratic elites, von Moltke ensured that entry was opened up to a much wider social pool – and that promotion to higher rank was based on merit rather than birthright. So the troops could feel confident about the objectives they were given.

At the same time, he introduced rigorous training at every level of the army. Not just parade ground discipline and bayonet practice, but tactics, role-playing, decision-making: what to do in different scenarios. Elements which, in other armies, were still regarded as the unique preserve of the officer class.

The result was that, in the chaos of battle, German soldiers were consistently able to make good decisions, because they knew what to do and they were confident in their ability to do it.

How you set people up to make good decisions

None of this is unique to the German army, of course. If you look at any high-performing team, you'll find strikingly similar characteristics.

The Danish restaurant Noma has been named the world's best for four of the last six years. Talented young chefs – many of them unpaid volunteers – are attracted both by Noma's reputation and by its culture of creativity. Every week's menu includes new dishes invented in the restaurant's test kitchen, where chefs will linger long into the night, excitedly trying out new flavour combinations.

Everybody who works there knows that it's not about the money: it's about the food. Or rather, it's about the experience of the food. For many diners, the most memorable part of a visit to Noma is the warmth of the welcome: the lack of pretension, the genuine love of eating.

There's a refreshing lack of hierarchy, with no distinction between front of house and kitchen: the person who serves your meal will also have helped to prepare it. Those who contribute to the restaurant are rewarded with partnership, including Ali Sonko, Noma's longstanding dishwasher, whose constantly cheerful demeanour was highlighted by founder Rene Redzepi as an essential factor in making it such a great place to work – and hence, such a great place to eat.

Then there's Nordstrom, the US department store, whose

reputation for world-class service has been built on a very clear ambition, backed up by constant examples of what good looks like – and uncompromising support for employees who try to do the right thing for customers, even when it may cost the business money in the short-term.

And then there are the All Blacks, New Zealand's iconic rugby union team. In November 2013, the All Blacks were losing a test match to a fired-up Ireland team: with 80 minutes gone, they were camped deep in their own half. They had to score, but time had run out: they knew the next time they made a mistake or gave away possession, the match would be over – and, with it, their 13-match winning streak. The pressure was extraordinary – and the temptation would have been to try something wild and desperate: a last throw of the dice to get them up the other end and conjure a winning score.

Instead, they just kept doing the basics: pass, catch, ruck, repeat, gradually inching their way up the pitch. Even without the pressure and full-time fatigue, you might expect a top-class international side to repeat that cycle four or five times before they made a mistake. The All Blacks did it ten times. They ground their way up the pitch, they forced the opening, they scored and they won.

And what makes it particularly interesting is that, despite the odds being stacked against them, nobody in the stadium was really surprised at the outcome – because the All Blacks' brand has been built on their ability, time after time, to execute accurately under pressure.

I've deliberately used examples that come from very different fields: fighting, cooking, retail, sport. And yet all of them exemplify the same characteristics we identified earlier:

Clarity about the outcome you're trying to achieve.

Confidence in your training and ability.

Trust in your leaders and in your team-mates.

These are the characteristics that make it easy for people to make good decisions and for organisations to work with minimum spec leadership.

So, what happens if you work in an organisation that doesn't yet work at this level? How can you use communication to change a process-driven culture into an empowered one? How can you inject those characteristics of clarity, confidence and trust?

Freedom within a framework

Everybody's heard of McDonalds; most people have an opinion about it. Which is why it makes such a fascinating example of what happens when a business that runs on process suddenly finds the wheels coming off.

For McDonalds in the UK, that moment was 2003. Up until then, the business had been growing steadily and profitably. The model was easy: every time they opened a new restaurant, new customers poured in and sales and profits went up.

But, as the new millennium dawned, it became clear that something had changed. McDonalds continued to invest in new restaurant openings, but the sales weren't going up any more – and, with investment costs rising, that was starting to hurt the bottom line.

Worse than that, the McDonalds brand seemed to have lost its magic touch with consumers. Negative headlines linking McDonalds to deforestation in Latin America were compounded with headlines about the 'McLibel' trial – with the firm being portrayed as a corporate bully. 'McJob' had become a derisory shorthand for a poor career choice.

The brand just seemed to be out of step – and looking increasingly irrelevant and out-dated in a world where more sophisticated and distinctive fast food options were popping up all over the place.

Nick Hindle was UK Communications Director for McDonalds at the time.

'We had a system that had always worked,' he says. 'And we became really, really good at executing it. Then, suddenly, the system wasn't working any more – and that was terrifying.'

The board realised they needed to make some radical changes. The first – and most important – was to stop paying lip-service to the idea of being customer-centric and make it a reality.

'We were what I'd call a DRIP business', says Hindle. 'Data rich, but insight poor. We were used to seeing the world through our own eyes, so our customer research focused on what people were saying about us – which was mostly just a snapshot of what we already knew: it might help us to tweak the menu or identify a service issue, but it didn't tell us anything about how we needed to evolve. We realised it was much more helpful to focus on what they were saying about other restaurants, other shopping experiences.'

The second big change was in the way McDonalds' leadership team communicated that customer message to the rest of the business, including the franchisees who run many of the restaurants.

'When you're going through a big change, everyone's got a lot to do, so it's tempting to drop communication lower down the priority list. But, in fact, what we realised is that you have to communicate more, not less. You have to bring people with you on the journey: that means getting them involved and being consistent in what you're telling them.'

For a business like McDonalds, with its rigid structures and detailed operating systems, this represented a significant cultural shift.

'You can't make a change like this with command and control,' explains Hindle. 'We set out to give people a clear framework – and then give them the freedom to act within that framework. That meant being very clear about what we were doing and why. It meant always talking about the business through our customers' eyes and always using the language they used. Customers trumped every other consideration – and, once people got used to that idea, it made it easy for them to make decisions at a local level.'

Not everything went swimmingly: there were some false starts along the way (you might remember the unspectacular foray into salads, for example). But, over the next few years, McDonalds successfully reinvented itself in the UK. Sales went up, profits went up – and customer perception studies showed that the brand had made itself feel relevant to a whole new generation.

A process-driven business managed to turn itself into a customer-centric business, simply by changing the way it communicated with its people.

Freedom to fail

Tucked away discreetly beside the Google campus in Mountain View, California is X, the internet giant's secret research laboratory.

This is where Google works on what it likes to call 'moonshots' – ideas big enough to have a genuinely transformative effect on the world and the way we live.

The X, by the way, stands for 'ten': not ten percent, but ten times. This is the scale of change that Google founder Larry Page is looking for when he talks about innovation – a philosophy he expanded on when interviewed for the January 2013 edition of *Wired* magazine:

'It's natural for people to want to work on things that they know aren't going to fail. But incremental improvement is guaranteed to be obsolete over time. Especially in technology, where you know there's going to be non-incremental change. So a big part of my job is to get people focused on things that are not just incremental.'

Since it was first set up in 2010, X has already turned a number of science fiction ideas into commercial reality. Some have stumbled: Google Glass, for instance (the augmented-reality eyewear), failed to achieve the mass acceptance it seemed destined for when first launched. A vertical farming project was shelved. And the jury's still out on self-driving cars. But what's remarkable about these – and the other high-profile projects in Google's pipeline – is the sheer scale of their ambition. They're BIG ideas.

The man charged with nurturing them to fruition is X's de facto head, Astro Teller (who, alongside his distinctively appropriate name, delights in the job title 'Captain of Moonshots' – perhaps the world's most enviable business card).

In a 2016 TED talk, Teller explained that one of the most important principles behind X is that it gives people freedom to fail: in fact, it rewards them for it.

'We work hard at X to make it safe to fail,' he says. Teams are encouraged to think big – and then encouraged to tackle the most challenging aspects of their project first, so that any potential drawbacks can be identified before too much time and money has been invested.

It's an intriguingly pragmatic approach to creativity: instead of being punished for disappointing results, teams are actively rewarded for killing their own ideas, because failing early means they can refocus their resources, rather than pursuing lost causes.

'Enthusiastic skepticism is not the enemy of optimism', says Teller. 'It's optimism's perfect partner.'

By making it safe to fail, Google has created an environment where people can be totally open about how things are working, which gives them the best possible chance of bringing extraordinary ideas to life.

In a nutshell...

#10 Learn to let go

Organisations agonise about the need to be 'agile', so they can respond to increasingly rapid changes in the market – but the reality is that large businesses tend to be bound up with process. The key to success is finding the right balance: giving people enough direction to know what to do – but not so much that it stops them thinking.

DO...

...treat your employees as grown-ups. Tell them the truth, listen to what they tell you and give them space to show what they can do.

DON'T...

...build a culture where people are afraid to make mistakes or express themselves openly. Freedom to fail is essential to creativity.

Making it happen

152 pages ago, we set out to explore how better internal communication could help your people make better decisions – and, in doing so, make your organisation feel more human and likeable.

We've identified the big issues that stop most internal communication from being effective. We've looked at examples of how different people and organisations have successfully overcome them. We've set out ten clear rules that will help.

And yet...

Nagging away at the back of your head, there's a 'but'.

'This is all quite interesting', you're thinking. 'I recognise the problems. I like the stories. I applaud the examples. But what can I actually *DO* with it?'

It's a fair question.

The glib answer would be: flip back to the end of each chapter and make sure you're doing all the things under the 'do' heading – and not doing the things under 'don't'.

But we both know it's not quite that simple.

Even if you happen to be the CEO of your company – and even if you recognise every one of the problems in this book – there's still a limit to how much you can do on your own.

So here's the longer and more complicated answer.

Changing the way an organisation communicates is not easy. If you want to shut down existing channels or open new ones, you'll need to elicit the support of the people who manage and run them, as well as their sponsors at the top of the business.

If you want to change the tone and style of your communication, you'll need to tread carefully and you'll need to consider the abilities of those involved. Not everyone will want to embrace a more human style of communication and not everyone will be able to: you can't expect someone who likes to express themselves in spreadsheets to become an engaging writer overnight. So, at least in the short-term, you'll have to find a way to resolve jarring inconsistencies in the way messages are expressed.

You'll need to bring your audience with you. People at every level of a business can be wary of change and, while they might welcome a more human tone in your communication, they may also wonder what's behind it. You can't expect to establish authenticity overnight: you have to earn their trust by being consistently open – even when they're asking awkward questions.

You'll also have to figure out a way of involving them more that doesn't feel either gimmicky or chaotic. Simply switching on a social media channel is not enough. You have to give people reasons to want to use it. You have to prompt them, encourage them, provide examples; above all, you absolutely have to respond to them.

And, somehow, you'll need to do all this without disrupting the day-to-day operation of the business. You can't just stop communicating: you have to figure out a way to change the wheels while you're driving the car.

So, no, it won't be easy.

But it can be done. And the way to start is by looking at how the internal communication works (or doesn't work) in your organisation.

You have to speak with one voice

Most businesses are quite careful about how they manage their communication externally.

They know exactly how many press officers they have, what they're saying and to whom. There are strict guidelines about who's allowed to speak to the press and what they're allowed to say.

But, on the inside, the story is often quite different.

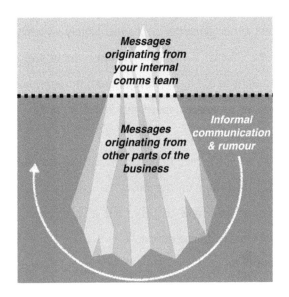

Internal communication in most organisations works a bit like an iceberg. On the surface, you've got the official channels managed by your comms team: the intranet, the town-halls, the conference, the newsletter, the change campaigns.

If you look beneath the surface, there's usually a much larger - and less structured - group of people who are also busy communicating to your employees. This might be a project manager who wants to get people engaged with a new product launch or a strategic change initiative. It might be a team leader or manager running a local town-hall meeting. It might be a Director's PA, who's been told to raise the profile of his or her area of the business.

Imagine if you ran your PR or advertising that way – giving anybody who fancied it a licence to talk to the media, or tweet random thoughts, or run their own little customer campaigns, with a confusing mish-mash of messages, language and graphic styles.

That would be crazy, wouldn't it?

And yet, that's exactly what happens on the inside of most organisations. Very few of them apply the same level of governance and consistency to their internal communication that they insist on externally.

More likely, messages will be haphazard and occasionally contradictory.

Different communicators will emphasise different priorities, depending on which agenda they're trying to promote or suppress. They will use a variety of channels – some official, some unofficial – as they jockey for a share of attention. The language, tone and presentation will vary tremendously.

This all feels very confusing and disjointed to their employees, who find it hard to decipher how everything fits together and which priorities they should be concentrating on. They feel less confident that they're working as part of a cohesive team.

The result is that they learn to tune out the 'official' channels and, instead, give far more weight to the information and opinions they glean from colleagues informally. Which is why the vast majority of communication in most organisations is based on informal conversations and rumour. After any major announcement, the first reaction of most employees is to talk it over with their colleagues, because that's the only way they think they'll get an interpretation they can trust.

So, how can you change that?

You have to start at the top

Over the last ten years, internal communication has grown rapidly as a business activity, but that growth has been allowed to happen in a random and haphazard way.

In a 2014 survey by Gatehouse Publishing, 64% of the respondents (all of whom work in internal communication roles for major organisations) said their organisation had no coherent internal communication strategy. In other words, communication was seen largely as a reactive function – a way to report the big decisions after they'd been taken, rather than a way of shaping the future. Only 53% agreed that internal communicators and senior leaders were on the same wavelength.

That's staggering. Can you imagine any organisation that would admit to not having a coherent marketing strategy? Or commercial strategy? Can you imagine any business succeeding if the Marketing Director disagreed with some of the other Directors about how to present the brand – and those other Directors all just went off and ran their own advertising and PR campaigns? What impression would you expect that to make on your customers?

It's absurd – and yet it's precisely what happens on the inside of most organisations every day.

That's why the single most important thing you can do to improve your internal communication is to make sure it's managed in a more coherent and joined-up way. That means consistency in language and tone. It means clarity about what the priorities are and how they are articulated. It means that, if you do have different teams in charge of different aspects of your communication, they need to work together and they need to report to the same place.

It means, above all, that communication needs to have a strong, single voice around the boardroom table: it has to be part of the planning, not just a mouthpiece trying to make retrospective sense of that plan.

If this is not how things are set up in your organisation at the moment, then you may well find that changing the status quo is not easy. This is because people have become used to the idea that internal communication is a bit of a free-for-all – that, if they're not happy with the way existing channels work, they can simply set up their own.

That's the thing with internal communication: even though people broadly understand that it's important, they very rarely think of it as something that needs to be taken seriously.

Which is a dangerous – and potentially fatal – mistake.

If I were an investment fund manager, one of the first things I would look at, when deciding whether to invest in a business or not, is its internal communication.

If a business is *not* set up to communicate well internally, it's unlikely to be able to adapt well to market changes, it's unlikely to deliver a consistently good customer experience – and it's always likely to be at risk of a reputation scandal.

In other words, it's not likely to be a very good long-term investment.

Does that thought worry you?

Perhaps not.

Perhaps your business is one of the 36% that has a coherent internal communication strategy – and one of the 28% where the CEO feels confident the internal communication is working.

Perhaps you look around you and you don't see dull presentations, inconsistent messages or people following mechanistic processes regardless of their outcome.

Perhaps there's not too much noise and no-one has the slightest doubt about what matters most.

Perhaps you're confident that the decisions your people take every day will be good ones.

Perhaps you never see or hear things in your organisation that make you think 'I'm glad our customers don't know about this.'

Perhaps everything is fine.

In which case, congratulations: you're one of the lucky ones.

Until you can honestly look around you and agree with all those statements, though, you've got a problem. The people in your organisation will not make the good decisions that you need them to. And the experience your customers have will not live up to the promises you make.

The only way to fix this problem is by changing the way you communicate on the inside.

And the only way to do that effectively is with the explicit involvement and commitment of the people at the very top of your organisation.

Are you going to tell them, or shall I?

The author

*Matt Hampshire is a partner in **mk**, one of the UK's best known internal communication agencies.*

He has spent over 25 years in communication, including early spells in advertising and PR.

He has worked in ten different countries, advised many of the world's leading companies and won more than 30 major national and international awards.

He now specialises in leadership communication, advising senior executives about how to develop and deliver more effective messages.

When he gets drunk, he likes to boast that he once played international rugby.

He is careful not to say who for.

https://matthampshire.blog

Lightning Source UK Ltd.
Milton Keynes UK
UKHW02f1915030518
322076UK00003B/18/P